The Tired
Country Smiles

O those hills, those beautiful hills,
How I love those Kentucky hills!
If on land or sea I roam
Still I think of happy home,
And those friends and loved ones
In those old Kentucky hills.

The Tired Country Smiles

by Nola Pease VanderMeer

with Frederick L. Luddy

HARLO PRESS/DETROIT

Library of Congress Catalog Card No.: 83-81475

ISBN: 0-8187-0053-X

Printed by Harlo Press, 50 Victor, Detroit, Michigan 48203

The seed for this story was planted many years ago. It has been watered and cared for

by my mother and father

by an organist in a little country church in Rush City, Minnesota

by many friends

by my beloved neighbors at Wooton's Creek and Morris Fork

. . . and by my husband, Samuel, so staunch and vibrant in his faith

To Him who has given me these many blessings and who has given us all a message of hope and joy . . .

This offering is made, with loving thanks to all who helped.

It seemed a tired country.

In every tired cabin there were tired mothers and undernourished children.

Even the cows looked too tired to continue giving milk . . . tired of the old nubbins.

The tired gates were off their hinges, and the tired soil was just hanging on the hillsides. The fences were so tired most of them had just dropped down.

The people were tired . . . tired of whiskey and violence, tired of trying to make a living on their worn out hillside farms.

—Sam VanderMeer

I recall driving down to see Uncle Sam and Aunt Nola shortly before they finished their year at the Farm School in North Carolina and went back to Morris Fork. It was just after the end of the major league season that year.

I remember that I was driving a rather snappy new yellow convertible that had been presented to me by the Buick people at General Motors. Some of the other players who were selected—those who were married—were recognized with sedans. Joe DiMaggio and I were the only bachelors and were given convertibles.

When I had pulled into the yard of the place where Uncle Sam and Aunt Nola were staying, Uncle Sam said, "Whew, it must be wonderful to live like that with all those fans!"

"Well," I said, "I guess I do have some fans, but the fame is fleeting. One day they cheer—the next they don't. You know, I think your pitching for the Lord, Uncle Sam, will last a lot longer than my pitching for the Reds."

—Johnny VanderMeer

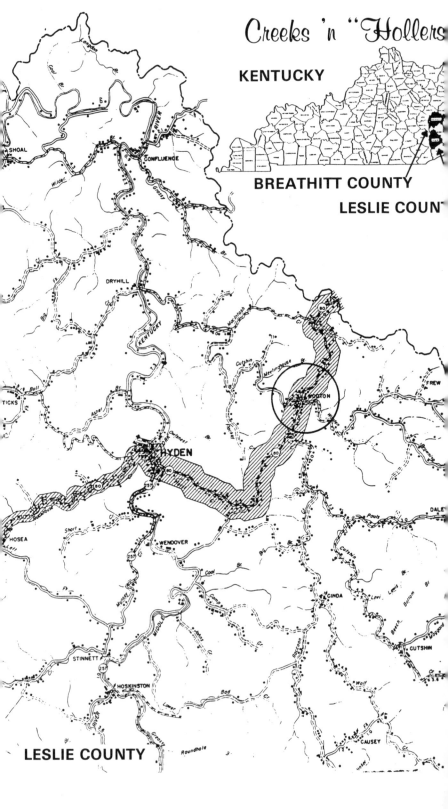

Creeks 'n "Hollers"

KENTUCKY

BREATHITT COUNTY

LESLIE COUN

LESLIE COUNTY

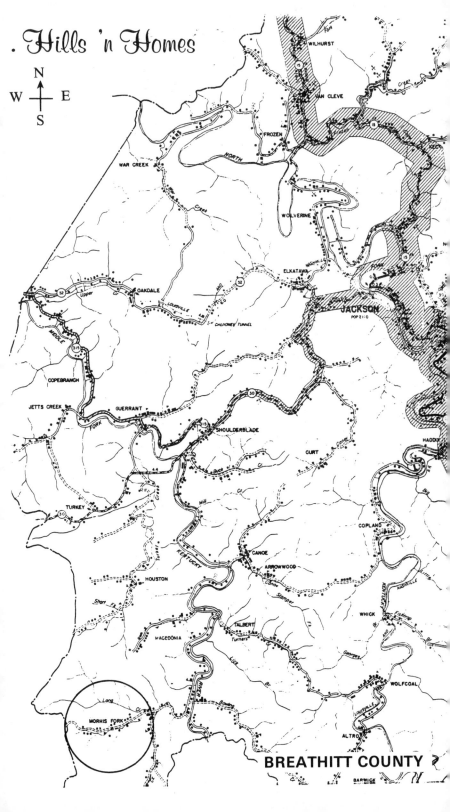

1

"I knowed you knowed what you knowed"

It had been quite a trek, horseback—through creeks and over steep mountain trails—to the little cabin way up the hollow.

The call had come around midnight. Someone was needed for a confinement case. Fresh in Appalachia, from my nurse's training in Illinois, there I was . . . the one to receive it.

"Hello—hello—hello. Is there someone there? My woman's sick—she needs a doctor nurse. Hello! Can anyone hear me?"

In my half sleepy stupor, I stumbled from my bed as the call penetrated the darkness—Who in the world, I thought—this time of night—What is the matter? But Miss McCord was more alert than I. I saw the small flame of the kerosene lamp in her room and heard her voice. "Yes—yes—there's someone here, come in."

Quickly stirring up the dying fire in the grate and slipping into her robe, she opened the door.

"Who are you?" she asked. "What's the trouble—someone sick? Come in."

"Yes," the stranger said. "My wife is goin to have a baby. Someone told me there was a doctor nurse who would help us. We need help bad."

"There is a nurse here. I'll call her, but she's not a

doctor—'' I dressed quickly as I listened to the conversation.

As I came into the room, the man turned to me, saying, "My wife's goin to have a baby—Someone told me you'd come to help. I hope you will. Better hurry; she's bad off."

Looking at the man in amazement, almost intuitively I asked, "What doctor are you going to have?"

"Why, they ain't no doctor," he replied. "That's why I come for you."

I took Miss McCord's hand, and we walked back to the bedroom. In a very frightened voice, I said, "I don't know what to do—I've never delivered a baby. We always had a doctor at the hospital—that was his job. Who will be there if I don't go?"

"Just neighbors," she replied. "But if you feel you can't do it, I won't insist."

"Well," I answered, a bit calmer, "guess I know as much as the neighbors would. If the Lord will help me."

We knelt by the bed, asking for guidance and help from the Great Physician in this, my first "case" in Appalachia!

I hurriedly packed what I thought would be "necessities" in my brand new saddle pockets while the man saddled my Dixie. Taking the lighted lantern from Miss McCord, I followed him to the barn. In a very few minutes, I was perched in the saddle. Then I was off . . . off, with a strange man, in a strange land, in the cold and darkness of a November night, going I knew not where!

I couldn't help being fearful as I clutched the handle of my lantern and tried to keep my place in the saddle. It was hard to see and follow in the darkness. Jogging through creeks and climbing up and down the mountain trails, we went along paths entirely foreign to me. This was my very first horseback ride ever! But Dixie was a "knowing animal" I had fed and petted . . . and had even saddled for practice a few times.

There was much silent prayer on that hour-long ride and not very much conversation, for my man (who told me he was "Mose") was not very loquacious. But I was inquisitive and wanted to know more of where I was going and what was expected.

"We're just poor folks around here," Mose explained. "We need friends—people who can help us. I shore am glad my neighbor knew about you and that you are willing to help." And not long after these few words, he said, "Well, here we are."

We dismounted and climbed a small hill. I was able to catch a glimpse of a lamp in a window. Breathing yet another silent prayer, I followed my man to the flickering light in the window.

Entering the cabin door, I found several neighbors in its one small room and at least a cheery fire in the fireplace. The mother-to-be sat, fully clothed, in a chair. Looking around, trying not to be too obvious, I spied a black kettle on the hearth. "My sterilizer," I thought jubilantly.

Going to my patient, I took her hand, introduced myself and began talking. We were soon acquainted. She told me her name was Martha.

"How many children do you have, Martha?"

"This will be number nine."

Whew! I thought, trying not to be too shocked or surprised.

Taking a nightie out of my saddle bags, I said to her, "Let me help you out of your clothes. You can put this on and lie down."

"Oh, I ain't never been to bed with any o' my babies," she said. "I always sit in a chair, in someone's lap." What next, I asked myself.

Neighbors continued to arrive, both men and women. Having a baby seemed to be an event with everybody interested and wanting to help. With the help of these neighbors, I finally persuaded the mother to lie down in the luxury of the clean nightie I had brought along. I busied myself, making what preparations I could . . . all the while with visions of our Blessing Hospital delivery room and all its equipment back home in Illinois.

15

As I boiled water in the black kettle, over the fireplace, how I did long for just a bit of that "necessary equipment" and the skilled hands of a Blessing Hospital M.D.!

In spite of the "innovation" of going to bed to have a baby and of other new and different suggestions, the mother was helpful. Her friendly neighbors counseled her to do as I asked. All seemed well. How I did appreciate the confidence of these new-found friends!

The long hours of the night passed, and just about daylight a beautiful little ten-pound baby boy arrived. With glad thanksgiving, I assured the folks that the Lord had indeed helped us.

As I cared for mother and babe, there was much getting acquainted conversation all around. I stayed until I knew all was well and promised to come back the next day.

As Mose was helping me on Dixie, he said, "Shore am glad you came tonight and did everything you did. I wanted you to come 'cause I knowed you knowed what you knowed."

I almost wept. Such gratitude and such confidence, coming to me from this stranger. What compensations there are in this world besides dollars and cents, I thought. The beauty, the value of new and trusting friends.

I knew now why I had come to the mountains.

2

Preparing for "China"

My Midwestern Girlhood
1893-1917

As a minister's daughter, my childhood had varied ac-
tivities and experiences. My father was English. He had
had most of his theological education in England, coming
to America to "finish up." Here he met and married a
southern Illinois girl. His first pastorate was in a Con-
gregational church in St. Clair, Michigan, where I was
born.

Many happy memories of those early days still cling,
along with the Christian guidance and teaching of my
parents. Both were strict regarding Bible teaching—and
not only teaching, but putting these teachings into every-
day practice.

We were taught especially that the Sabbath was the
Lord's day for His service and worship. None of our other
weekly activities was allowed on Sunday. Our Sunday ac-
tually began on Saturday, with extra cooking, house
cleaning, "getting the children ready," and other
necessary preparations. We had our Sunday dinner on
Saturday night, with always enough extra prepared for
our Sunday meal. Would my mother stay home from
church to "fix a nice dinner for visitors?" No indeed! We
children—six of us ultimately—were marched to Sunday
School and the morning service every Sabbath day.

I can still see sixteen shoes in a row on our kitchen

floor, all polished by my father, ready for Sunday services.

Then there were Christian Endeavor and churchnight services for different age groups in the evening. As we gradually grew into our school program, with its regular activities, we grew also into the church program with its activities, and all its services. "These are just as important as your school work," preached my father.

While I was still very young, our family moved to South St. Paul, Minnesota. One of the biggest joys of life thereabouts was skating and sledding. As I grew old enough, I longed for my own skates. One Christmas, I was sure they would come, as I'd made this desire for just one Christmas present well known.

I could hardly wait to get my package from under the tree. Opening it—I found a lovely . . . leather Bible! I hardly knew what to say, my disappointment was so keen. "Getting ready for Eternity is just as important as learning to skate," said my father. "I hope you will like your Bible. Read it and obey it."

I have surely heeded his request, but have wished many times also that I had learned how to skate—and with a nice new pair of skates!

Still, they were wonderfully happy days, even those that brought the thirty to forty degree below zero weather. I learned the joys of ice and snow (even without skates!) and did not bemoan any of the handicaps of such a frigid climate.

We walked to and from school—no matter what the distance or weather, unless we could catch a ride on the bobsleds that hauled manure from the St. Paul stockyards to the various farms close by. This was great fun. We would hang onto the runners, inhaling the "manure perfume," while hitching as far as we could. Many times Jack Frost would nip the ears, or the tip of the nose. But this was "cured" as soon as we reached school and the teacher took us outside and washed the frosted areas with snow. We would soon "thaw out" and go back to our studies.

Skating and sledding parties filled much of the time

that children and families always seemed to find to get together. Church activities were an important part of our lives. Usually there were four services on Sunday, weekly "prayer meetings," and numerous dinners, suppers and parties at the church. I remember one night going to a church supper when suddenly the heavens became a glowing, red flame and the sky seemed to rock back and forth! A bunch of frightened children, not recognizing the Aurora Borealis, began screaming, "It's the end of the world, the end of the world!" and ran wildly into the church. Then we learned that these northern lights were very common in this part of the country. Thereafter we just enjoyed the beauty and wonder of them.

I remember just as distinctly a severe storm that came up during school hours when I was in the second or third grade. Heavy thunder and intense lightning were everywhere. We were about frightened out of our seats. Then, in utter calmness, our teacher said, "Let's all go stand by the window and watch the storm. I want you to see the lightning God is showing us; I want you to hear His rolling thunder." Up from our seats we jumped, following our teacher across the room. We gazed in awe at the storm, talking and laughing, with no sign of fear. "Soon we'll see the beautiful rainbow," our teacher said. "God has put that there so we can remember His promise that He'll never destroy the earth by flood."

All through the years this incident has been a part of my life. It has taught me that there need be no panic in our lives . . . if we will just listen to what God tells us. I have had no fear of storms ever since.

When I was in high school in Mount Sterling, Illinois, my mother became very ill with pneumonia. In those days, hospital care was almost unheard of, so our doctor secured a nurse to come to our home to care for her. This nurse became my idol!

How beautiful she was in her stiff, white uniform, as she bustled about quietly, day and night, doing things that helped to make my mother well. I so admired her dedication and ability, that I wondered if I could ever do some of the things she did. When I talked to her about becoming a nurse, she encouraged me and told me about Blessing Hospital in Quincy, just a few hours away.

After my mother's recovery, we often talked of Miss Glindeman and of the wonderful ways she had helped. I told my mother that I wanted to be a nurse. She was somewhat aghast at the thought. "I don't know too much about it," she said, "but if that's what you want to do, your father and I will help you all we can after you finish high school. I'm afraid it's very hard and demanding work, although with the Lord's help you can do it—if you really want to. But three years is such a long time for you to be away!"

Soon after high school commencement, I was accepted as a "probe" in Blessing Hospital. In those days, we were probationers for the first six months, just to see how we "fitted in" and if the hospital wanted to continue our training.

Much to my surprise, my mother said she was going to accompany me on the train from Mt. Sterling to Quincy. I suppose it was because although I was the oldest of six, I was the first to leave the nest. We arrived in Quincy quite late in the afternoon. As I was looking for a way to get to the hospital, Mother said, "I want to go somewhere else first." She found the address of a Presbyterian minister, and we went directly to his house! Introducing us, she said, "This is my daughter, Nola. She is going to study nursing at Blessing Hospital. She'll be here for three years, and I want you, please, to take care of her. She's never been away from home. She will come to your church, so please help her all you can. I am leaving her in your care."

And so Dr. Hartley took me under his good Presbyterian wing. I became as active as possible in the church life, although I soon learned that sick folks had to be cared for on Sundays as well as Mondays! On my free Sundays, I was usually able to get to the church for the evening activities of Christian Endeavor. They were just like the ones I'd been "brought up with" at home. It was through

Christian Endeavor Life Work Recruits that I really became interested in missionary service, and in offering my life to Christ as His recruit.

After the three years of my nurse's training, I received a commission from our Presbyterian Board of Foreign Missions. How excited I was at the real prospect of going to China as a medical missionary!

I was fully ready to depart in 1917, but with war conditions, the Board was unable to implement its plans for me and for others. Then suddenly a request came from the Kentucky mountains. A nurse was apparently needed there in a new project just begun by our National Board of Home Missions. Would I be willing to come? In correspondence with both Foreign and Home Boards, the Foreign Board consented to "loan" me to the Home Board for a year, or until I could safely go to China. The course of more than a half century of my life was to be changed. But how much, I could not yet know.

As the early autumn days passed, the sudden prospect of going to the strange land of the Kentucky mountains was no less exciting than the earlier prospect of going to the strange land of China. I knew nothing of the mountain people nor of their real needs. And there was not time or way in which to learn quickly enough. I knew only that my new home would be at Wooton's Creek, a hundred miles or so southeast of Lexington.

I gathered my world together somehow, said very heartfelt goodbyes to my family and boarded the train at Bloomington—for Lexington and all that was beyond.

As the miles passed, the familiar faded behind me, and the unfamiliar unfolded ahead. Prayerful thoughts and wonderment filled me. . . . Then, after a time, a calmness of soul. As we came closer to Kentucky, I became eager to meet whatever lay ahead.

In Lexington, there were instructions to come to Typo, via the L. & N. train; there I would be met with a wagon for the trip to Wooton. My eyes bulged a bit more and my breath came a bit faster. To be met by a wagon? I'd never had a wagon ride. Who would meet me? How would I know him? How long a ride would it be?

By nine o'clock the next morning—a bright, Kentucky day—I met the L&N train and we were off, right on schedule. What a train ride! Chandeliers of kerosene lamps shook back and forth on the ceiling, a potbellied stove sat in the center of an aisle. There were open windows and no screens. As we whistled and wound our way along, deep clouds of smoke and soot poured through the windows, right into our faces. There were many stops along the crooked mountain tracks. Friends greeted friends, getting off and on. There really were no stations—just "stopping off" places. Houses were few and far between. There were no roads, and no cars, not ONE in sight anywhere along the entire journey.

As we chugged deeper and deeper into the mountains and it seemed we were really leaving civilization behind, I sank deeper and deeper into thought. The great beauty on every side was most amazing—the tall mountains, heavily wooded with almost every kind of tree, all painted in the most gorgeous colors. The October beauty thrilled and awed me. I had never dreamed of seeing anything like it. How can I tell my folks about it, I wondered.

Completely lost in thought, trying to drink in all the wonder around me, I was brought back to earth suddenly when the conductor called, "Typo, Typo!" It was about two o'clock in the afternoon. Half dazed, I began gathering my things together, and as the train jerked to a halt, I wondered, what next! As I climbed down the steps, a strange man came up to me. "You Miss Pease?" he asked. Before I could reply, he continued, "I'm Albert Brewer. Miss McCord sent me to fetch you; here's a note from her." Trying to get my balance on the little rocky path and forcing a smile to avoid looking too bewildered, I took the note. "Sure am glad to see you, Mr. Brewer!" I remarked. With that he went on, "If you're ready, we'd better go— hit's quite a fur piece. My mules are sorta slow, and I'd like to get home by feedin' time. My wagon's right over there. Oh, here, Miss McCord sent you some lunch." I asked him to please see about my trunk, and while he did, I took a minute to read the note. *"This is Mr. Brewer. He will bring you to Wooton in his wagon. There's nothing to be afraid of. There will be no place to get anything to eat, so I fixed you just a bite of lunch. We'll be waiting for you—don't worry about a thing."*

Again I drank in more of the beauty of the wonderful mountains surrounding us, and collected my hand baggage for the wagon.

Still there were no cars, no highways, and hardly a person in sight. A few horses and mules were hitched here and there, but somehow it hadn't become clear to me that this was mountain transportation! Breathing a fervent prayer, I followed Mr. Brewer to his wagon where the mule team was hitched to a small tree by the river. As he tossed my "stuff" into it, I looked around, saying, "How are we going to get across the river? I don't see any bridge." "Oh, they ain't no bridge, never was one here. We just ford the river." In almost a trance, and with his help, I "histed" myself into the wagon. He untied the mules, jumped in and, with a slap of the reins, we splashed into the river.

Very nonchalantly, the mules picked their way, and I realized that although this was my first such venture, it was not theirs. Clutching my purse and my lunch, and trying to hold on to the side of the wagon, I suddenly missed my watch from my wrist. "Oh, Mr. Brewer!" I screamed. "I've lost my watch!" In some unguarded moment, it had slipped from my arm—this special gift of my mother and father for my graduation. I could hardly hold back the tears. "Whoa, whoa!" he called to his mules. Before I knew what was happening, he was into the river, wading up and down on each side of the wagon, searching the river bottom with hands as well as boots. "Well, I am sorry—don't seem to find it. Guess we'll have to get on . . . " Soaking wet, he got slowly back into the wagon. My lovely watch—gone. But the hurt of losing it was softened by this marvelous act of friendliness, his doing all he could to help, undaunted by the chilly wading and an uncomfortable ride home in wet clothes! And all this for me, a perfect stranger, a person he'd never seen before.

Such a ride! We did indeed ford the river and safely reach the other side. There the thirteen miles of mountain travel really began. What a trail—up the sides of some mountains, and down others, through many, many creeks. Everywhere were the big tall trees with their unbelievable maze of color, the golds and browns and reds, mixed with the different shades of green of several species of pine. "I've never seen anything so beautiful as these mountains," I said to Mr. Brewer. "Aren't they grand? How long have you been here?" "Yep," he replied. "They are purty. I've been here forever—don't know nuthin different. Glad you like 'em!"

Becoming accustomed to the scenery, I found more questions to ask. "Where are the people? I just don't see anybody around. How do they live, way out like this? I don't see any factories or any place where folks can work." "Oh, we make it," he answered, "though sometimes it's pretty rough. But we have our farms— gardens—cows and pigs and chickens. That's about all we need. Right now most of the farms are sorta wore out . . . I wish we could do more for our younguns. Sometimes I think it ain't much of a life for them. I wish somebody who knew how—knew what we need—could come out here and help us."

Little by little, the miles passed, with only occasional conversation. Several times I almost rolled off the seat. The sounds of the wagon wheels, the trickling of the creeks as we went up and down the hills, the bumps over the rocks, the wonderful mountain sunshine and the coolness of the October day with all its beauty filled my soul. Every "twice in a while," Mr. Brewer would urge his mules on a bit with a touch of the whip. Then, as we were climbing up one small hill, he announced: "Well, this is 'ooton's Creek, and there's your house . . . And there's Miss McCord!"

24

3
Wooton's Creek
1917-1927

Mary Rose McCord had come to Wooton's Creek the March before. A consecrated Christian, with a vision and a great longing to help others, Miss McCord had been working in a girls' school in Mt. Vernon, Kentucky. She was just turning it over to other hands who could take care of it, when she heard of Wooton's Creek. She had earlier been on the faculty of Jacksonville College for Women in Illinois. From these experiences, she was thoroughly prepared to assume the inspirational leadership of a project which included religious, educational and social development in a community that had lived from year to year without it. As she came to greet me, her lovely face was aglow. "Welcome to Wooton and our mountains. We are so happy you are here. Come into the little home we have fashioned for ourselves here in the hills. We are trying to make it comfortable and livable. Mr. Brewer will help carry your things." I knew immediately that I was going to love my new home.

"How wonderful," I said. "It was such a beautiful drive. Thank you, Mr. Brewer, for the trip."

He smiled and replied, "Well, I'll see you again. Am glad yer here. Hope you'll like it."

It didn't take me long to feel at home in the little room Miss McCord showed me. "This little house," she said, "was here all along. How we scrubbed and cleaned it.

A stop in my Wooton rounds.

Then some of the men added these two little rooms—they just cut some lumber from the hills and built them. We kalsomined the ceiling and walls. Isn't it pretty?'' Indeed it was. How a bit of energy and imagination had transformed a dreary ''no good'' cabin.

Later, we talked around a glowing fire in the fireplace—the only source of heat for the little cabin. ''I wanted to find a place where people really needed help,'' Miss McCord said. ''Some pioneer place where no one else had been, no missionary, I mean. My great grandmother was Nancy Rice, Mrs. Benjamin Spillman, from Kentucky, so I wanted to come to the Kentucky mountains.''

In Wooton's Creek, Miss McCord surely had found an isolated, pioneer spot. It lay deep in the southeastern part of Kentucky, in the heart of Appalachia. Its mountain folk were still pioneers—descendants of others before them who had migrated from Scotland, England, and Ireland. They emigrated beyond the first points of settlement, hopeful of finding greater freedom in the rugged, isolated hills, far, far removed from the rest of the world—from any civilization. So far removed were they, in fact, that they became a people unto themselves—shut off from contacts with anyone or anything outside of their hill country. After a century of such isolation, their land had grown tired. There was no industry of any sort and no contact with anything that was going on in the rest of the state, let alone the country. It was quickly clear to me that I had come to a land of the ''do without,'' with none of the ''necessary luxuries'' I had grown up with all my life. These mountain folks had struggled long. If they were to survive, they knew they must welcome help from somewhere. Slowly they opened their homes and hearts to those of us who came to them. And it was through the church that we had come, to make the first advances . . . to offer what we could of the life more abundant for these isolated and forgotten Americans.

Soon after I arrived, a neighbor said, ''I'd like to see that nurse.''

''Come right up,'' Miss McCord answered.

The inquisitive lady, who lived "down the hill" from our little cabin, came up the hill and looked me up and down. "Why, you ain't no different—you look just like one o' us!" And that was that. The barriers were down, and even though I was still "the fotched-on nurse," I soon found my place in this strange new world.

I had been at Wooton barely a year when something very exciting served to remind me of our isolation from our times and the world. I happened to be the one called upon to take a visitor from Wooton to Typo that late autumn day in 1918. Arriving at the little "road stop station," after crossing the river to come into Typo, I noticed there was more of a crowd than usual, and many folks talking excitedly. I could hear they were talking about the war. "Did you know the war was over?" someone asked. I was aghast—for with no radio, newspapers or telephone, we had not heard much of any news! Soon the train pulled in. I hastily ran to the conductor asking if he had a paper— "Sure have," he replied—"and it tells all about the ending of the war." I grabbed it, hastily taking in the headlines and bits of front page information. Sure enough, the war was over, but with no phones, no papers . . . no communication of this sort, we knew nothing about it until this moment!

I mounted Dixie and we forded the river again. I gave him a big pat, and off we went thru the dark, over those mountain trails. I sang all the way; first the Doxology, then the Star Spangled Banner. Even though the cabins were far apart, some taking me off the regular route home, I stopped at every one along the way, telling the wonderful news, "The War is over; the war is over!"

It was hard to realize at Wooton that we were a community at all—completely shut off as we were from the rest of the world. Our only roads were the creeks or the rough mountain paths here and there—our transportation was by horseback or wagon. And there was walking . . . aplenty of it.

The hillside farms with their meager crops provided the only nourishment there was. And these farms were wearing thin from constant cultivation. There was no rotation of crops, no knowledge of any kind of land improvement—no winter crops. Rough, homemade mule drawn plows and sleds were all the farm implements there were. The women worked side by side with their menfolk in the rough, hillside cornfields and did such family gardening as there was.

There were reports of rich minerals, especially coal, in the hills, but with such isolation, industry was impossible. The closest churches were in Hyden, Buckhorn, and Jackson, but these were too many hard, horseback miles away.

Wooton folks were hungry . . . mentally, physically and spiritually. Their once stalwart, pioneer spirit was now bedraggled and discouraged. Illiteracy was prevalent, with a lack of schools on every side. Surely, this was a place for life more abundant. With its promise of a brighter future, the folks responded joyously and with great anticipation to a "missionary program" dedicated to this.

I remember to this day what one of my early friends at Wooton said about her grandchild. "Hit's got sense, but hit's got to learn how to use that sense." This seemed to me such a clear invitation to us to carry out our work . . . *"Diamonds do not lie so thick in nature as they do in Arabian Nights; they are rare, scattered . . . and miners must delve through masses of clay and rock before they light on these priceless gems."*

There was a real interest in having regular Sunday services. A minister had come from Hyden, a 12-mile horseback trip, perhaps once a month. But there had been no Sunday School, no organizations or opportunities for constructive Christian training. And so we began. We found a sadly dilapidated schoolhouse, just right for Miss McCord's "fix-up" spirit. But many times, because the response was enthusiastic, we found ourselves out under the trees. The little schoolhouse was not ample enough for the crowd of 100, sometimes more, who came. What prayerful planning for such a group! There was no source of "teachers" for our beginning—we had to divide the large group among three of us: Miss McCord, fellow worker Maud Rowlee, and myself. Some of our older folks soon "took hold," and our Sunday School staff grew.

Realizing that we needed to instill a community spirit so that all phases of life could be touched and "made new," Miss McCord organized the Wooton Improvement League. The League took in all our people . . . their needs, their projects. Here all "matters of state" were settled.

We attacked the school and illiteracy problem. Our little community school was so inadequate and uncertain. Many times there was no teacher and no school day. After considerable gentle persuasion, the League voted to have a "brought on" teacher, not a mountain person. Implementing this was a delicate subject for discussion with our County Superintendent in Hyden. Such a procedure was unheard of. But Miss McCord had a way, and soon she was allowed to secure the very competent services of a friend from Illinois. What an addition Alice Fry was to our little cabin family community! Alice was not only a real, honest to goodness teacher, who brought many needed and wonderful innovations to the little school; she was a wonderful musician also. Such a blessing and enrichment to all of us.

We soon found that "out stations" needed friendly help. These even smaller communities, within a three, four, and five mile radius, were isolated too. Because of the long horseback travel, they had little communication with each other. Upper and Lower McIntosh, Upper Cutshin, Flackey, Meeting House Branch, Upper and Lower Wooton Creeks—their folks welcomed the missionaries with their "help you" programs. There were mothers' groups, children's clubs, men's farming clubs. "Workings" were frequent. These involved the whole community coming forward to help with whatever the need or project of the hour might be. Much of this volunteer work redeemed the dishevelled schoolhouse that had seemed to be beyond redemption. There were road "workings"—when chug

30

holes were filled, rocks moved, and even some rough mountain "edges" removed to take the road up and out of the creek. In times of need, we helped each other with the gardens, the many small cornfields, the "stir offs" of sorghum molasses, the bean stringings, the corn shuckings, and even the apple parings. Mothers would get together to help each other with quiltings.

Everybody loved a "stir off." The molasses cane was grown in the fields with regular corn, and when ripe, was gathered and taken to as large a "flat bottom" as was available. For a day, the men would see to "squeezing the juice." This was accomplished primarily by a mule hitched to a "turning mill." The green stalks of sorghum cane were pushed into the mill, while the mule went round and round and round at the end of a long pole. As the corn stalks were squeezed, the sap would drip from them. Then it was collected, put in a large container, which was hung over a roaring fire. The sap "biled down" until it was thick and tasty molasses. A special hole was made for the bubbles and foam that would come to the top of the molasses. This would be skimmed off and poured in a scrap hole. Oftentimes such a hole would be cleverly covered with brush and branches, and some unsuspecting person would be guided there.

The good, rich molasses we had after these "stir offs"—how it helped our nutrition program. The mountain folk had had "stir offs" long before we came on the scene. They had been one of nature's ways of curing and staving off malnutrition.

Distant as we were from stores of any description, we did have to sometimes wonder where our food was coming from. How were we to get through the bad winter months? Although our hillsides and gardens—along with our neighbors'—supplied fresh fruit and vegetables for summer use and for canning, there were foods, especially in winter, we wanted very much to savor. But where could we obtain these? Joy be, we discovered Montgomery Ward had a food mail order department!

We discovered, too, that any groceries ordered had to

be ordered before our fall rains, which frequently brought floods, and before ice and snow that would prevent our "mail wagon" from running. This was an ordinary farm wagon, drawn by mules or horses, that provided our only parcel delivery across a dozen or more rugged miles.

Very early in October, we would begin to check our shelf supplies or "canned stuff," the Montgomery Ward catalogue, and our checkbook. Our order would include tea, coffee, cereals, dried fruits, fish, canned juices, and whatever other "goodies" we felt we needed—and could afford.

One cereal we were especially fond of, and could not secure elsewhere, was cracked wheat. This had to be cooked several hours. But, with our fireless cooker, that was no problem. It was a small metal cabinet, with two deep holes. In these were placed red hot soap stones, heated on a coal-burning stove. The cereal, with boiling water, was placed in aluminum cookers, sealed, and left on the hot soap stones. The cooker did its job beautifully. By 6 a.m., breakfast was ready. The delicious cereal had cooked all night, without electricity or fire. How thankful we were, in those early days, for Montgomery Ward!

But it was the ending note of an arduous expedition of the early Twenties which brought the preciousness of fresh beef home to me.

By this date in time, Hazard, the seat of neighboring Perry County, was already a growing city—at least for the mountains. A visit from Wooton, therefore, was a real event. At this time, there was no highway . . . only the usual dirt roads and mountain pathways. Even though it was an all-day horseback trip from Wooton, every so often we undertook it, just to see the sights and to obtain fresh and different groceries. Sometimes, if it were a rainy period, we'd ride right down Main Street with mud coming up to our stirrups and the horse's belly. On a winter visit, the stirrups would freeze!

Kindly Dr. Collins lived in Hazard. He and his family had become very good friends, asking me to visit any time I could come. I enjoyed so many good visits and many

CINCINNATI, LOUISVILLE, LEXINGTON, HAZARD AND McROBERTS

Additional Trains between Neon and McRoberts

	101 Daily	107 Ex.Su	103 Daily			102 Daily	108 Ex.Su	104 Daily
	AM	PM	PM	Lv. Neon, Ky. Ar		AM	PM	PM
	3 15	7 20	3 15	Lv. Neon, Ky. Ar		9 40	6 45	9 55
		7 29	3 26	Lv. Fleming Lv.		9 33		9 49
	3 33	7 35	3 35	Ar McRoberts, Ky. Lv		9 24	6 32	9 40
	PM	PM	AM			AM	PM	PM

d Nos. 1 and 3 will stop on signal at Montrose, Fenwick and Wyandotte to let off passengers from Louisville and beyond.

e No. 1 will stop at Avon to let off passengers from Louisville and beyond.

f Train stops on signal.

g Nos. 1 and 3 stop on signal on Sunday at Haddix, Coolidge and at stations between Jackson and Beattyville except Yeadon.

h Stops on signal on Sundays only.

i Meals.

Nos. 1, 2, 3 and 4 will stop on signal at Gamboe, Baker, Agawam, Mina, Sloan, Cressy, Harg, Wiseman Crossing, Calloway Crossing, Millers Creek, Lock No. 14, Willow, Yellow Rock and Belle Point.

Nos. 1, 2, 3, 4, 7 and 8 stop on signal at Napier, Butterfly, Combs, Cornettsville, Ulvah, Roxana, Ice and Sergent.

Nos. 3 and 4 stop on signal at White Ash.

Nos. 7 and 8 stop on signal at Alloway, Elko, Ermine, Whittaker.

Nos. 3, 4, 7 and 8 stop on signal at Chenocee, Ukatawa, Dumont, Wolfreal, Darwick, Dunraven, Conda, Domino, Lennut, Christopher, Blaklock, Glenaver, Stormking, Dakota, Bluefield, Uz, Whitco, Caudell and Bastin.

Nos. 7, 8, 181, 182, 307 and 308 stop on signal at Pelham, Montrose, Ware Crossing, Vanmeter, Kbross, Wattaca, Cardinham, Argyle, Virden, Shawanee, Airdale, Derrick and Loomis.

All trains between Hazard and Carbon Glow stop at Harther, Letcher, Duo and Lelly.

Table 40 — STURGEON CREEK BRANCH

	23 Ex.Su Mixed		24 Ex.Su Mixed
	AM	Lv. Heidelberg, Ky. Ar	PM
	8 00	Lv. Heidelberg, Ky. Ar	8 32
	8 05	Lv. Cortyon Lv.	8 22
	8 15	Ar Ida May, Ky. Lv	8 20

I Ex.Su | Train stops on signal.

Table 41 — CARRS FORK BRANCH

Trains stop on signal at Roan, Parlo, Happy, Shepherd, Agnes, Wiscoal, Scuddy, Montana and Green Ridge.

No. 7 leaves on Hazard and Jeff.

	121 Ex.Su	67 Mixed	Distance			68 Mixed	122 Ex.Su
	PM	AM		Lv. Hazard, Ky. Ar		AM	PM
	1 10	6 55	0	Lv. Hazard, Ky. Ar		10 55	
	1 15	7 00	1 0	Lv. Lothair Lv.		10 44	
	1 25	7 25	5 9	Lv. Jeff Lv.		10 15	3 20
	1 29	7 30	5 9	Lv. Jeff Ar		10 15	3 20
	1 45	7 55	10 4	Lv. Defiance Lv.		9 57	2 55
	2 27	9 12	14 5	Ar Emmons Lv.		9 13	2 28
	1 52	8 07	12 4	Ar Vicco Lv.		8 50	2 18
	1 53	8 10	12 4	Ar Sassafras Lv.		8 47	2 14
	2 03	8 29	11 9	Ar Anco, Ky. Lv		8 39	2 04

Table 42 — LOTS CREEK AND JAKES BRANCHES

Trains stop on signal at Wabaco, Hilton, Tauler, Fresey, Pioneer, Ajax, Ka Sa, and Tribley.

	234 Sun.	214 Ex.Su	224 Sun.	204 Ex.Su	Distance		200 Sun.	229 Ex.Su	219 Sun.	239 Sun.
	PM	PM	AM	AM		Lv. Hazard, Ky. Ar	AM	PM	PM	PM
	5 15	4 15	9 55	8 40	0	Lv. Hazard, Ky. Ar	10 25	11 40	6 00	7 00
	5 27	4 27	10 07	8 52	2 2	Lv. Allais Lv.	10 12	11 27	5 45	6 47
	5 40	4 40	10 20	9 05		Lv. Diablock Lv.	10 00	11 15	5 35	6 35
	5 48	4 48	10 28	9 13		Ar Pioneer No. 2 Lv.				
	5 49	4 49	10 29	9 14		Ar Pioneer No. 2 Lv.				
	6 17	5 17	10 57	9 42		Ar Hardburly, Ky Lv	9 43	10 58	5 18	6 18

Table 43 — FIRST CREEK BRANCH

All trains stop on signal at Lenard, Combs, Domino, German, Blue Diamond, Blue Diamond No. 2, Bonnyman, Windon, Clemons, and Hayden.

	230 Sun.	220 Sun.	210 Ex.Su	200 Sun.	Distance		203 Ex.Su	213 Sun.	223 Sun.	233 Sun.
	AM	AM	AM	AM		Lv. Hazard, Ky. Ar	AM	PM	PM	PM
	3 00	7 40	2 00		0	Lv. Hazard, Ky. Ar	8 30	4 05	9 45	5 05
	3 25	8 05	2 25		5 4	Lv. Typo Lv.	8 00	3 35	9 15	4 35
	3 30	8 10	2 30	6 55	5 4	Lv. Typo Ar	7 55	3 30	9 10	4 30
	3 50	8 30	2 50			Ar Harveyton, Ky. Lv	7 25	3 00	8 40	4 00
	AM	PM	AM				AM	PM	PM	PM

No. 200 starts from North Hazard 6 15 a m.

47   48

"Our" page from the L and N schedules book—circa 1920. Six hours plus from Lexington to Typo, and no express runs!

hearty meals in their home. At any time I needed him for an emergency, Dr. Collins would make the sixty-mile horseback trip from Hazard to Wooton and back—performing critical surgery on a homemade dining room table with the light of a kerosene lamp.

Coming to Wooton by the L. & N., we usually got off at Chavies. It was the closest station to us. But one time I went directly on to Hazard from Louisville. I had to board the train in Louisville at 7:30 a.m. in order to arrive in Hazard, less than 200 miles away, by 9:30 p.m.—14 hours later!

This night, of course, no one from Wooton would meet me. I had to wait until morning for my horse to come. There was one very small "hotel." Although I had no reservation, I went to it hopefully, because I knew the lady hotel keeper. "Oh, I'm so sorry," she said. "We don't have one empty room, but I'll let you stay with me tonight." I thanked her, and told her I was tired and hungry, as I began trying to sort out my baggage and parcels.

In a few minutes she came to me saying, "I just remembered, I have an empty room of a travelling man. He won't be here tonight, so you can have that."

"Are you sure he won't be back?" I asked, though I was quite overjoyed with the thought of having a whole hotel room all to myself for the night!

"Oh, no," she replied. "You'll be perfectly safe. I'll try to find you a bite to eat."

Carrying my luggage, I walked up the stairs to my second-floor room. 'Twas small, no closet, and men's possessions were everywhere. I turned down the covers. Of course, the bedding was not fresh. It was very late in the fall, quite coolish, so I kept my coat on and stretched out on top of the bed. Suddenly I thought, what if this man should come back tonight? I lighted my lamp, and with main force and considerable awkwardness, pulled the small dresser in front of the door, which had no lock! Part of the night I'd sit in the only chair, then lie down, coat and all, but *nary* a wink o' sleep came. 'Twas just beginning to get daylight, when I heard a shot. Someone raced up the stairs and tried to open my door! I tried not to scream, and with an earnest prayer kept a certain degree of composure. Nothing else happened—all became quiet. As soon as daylight came, I moved the dresser back, and went downstairs. "Just a drunken fight," my hostess said. "Didn't amount to anything."

I had a little wait before my horse came for the ride back to Wooton. Certain that all my upsets were over, I hied to the grocery.

At Wooton's Creek we never had beef. How I missed steaks and roasts! But 'twas always chicken or pork, which our people raised; sometimes, fish. So, thinking that just this once I might indulge myself, I bought three small steaks—one for each of us living in the community house at the time. The clerk was kind enough to wrap them several times, saying they'd keep okay for the thirty miles of my horseback trip home.

I arrived at Wooton a bit before nightfall; I could hardly wait to get the steaks out and give them to Mrs. Russell, who had charge of our "meal getting." I said, "Guess it's too late to have these for supper, but I was hungry for steak, so brought us a present—we can have 'em tomorrow."

When tomorrow's noon meal appeared, here came steaming bowls of soup!

"I knew we couldn't afford to eat those steaks in one meal, so I made soup—they'll last about a week this way," exclaimed our exuberant cook.

I excused myself quickly and ran to my room, so no one would see my tears!

All those horseback trips had made terribly clear the need for roads. What was the worth of building churches and schools—and programs or projects—if people couldn't get to them? Mules and wagons had seemed sufficient for just "shiftin' 'round," with nowhere special to go. But we were thirteen horseback miles from a railroad. The nearest hospital at Lexington meant a train trip of six to seven hours after this ride to Typo. It was dangerously time consuming, as well as expensive, for the small and often empty purses. Yet the mountains were part of Kentucky. Why couldn't we be "connected" with the other part?

Miss McCord had made some contact with the State Highway Department during her time in Mt. Vernon, and she resolved to maintain this for the sake of Leslie County. But it was a hard resolve to carry out. There was much, much correspondence, and much journeying to Frankfort and the State Highway Department offices there.

Becoming acquainted with Leslie County's Judge Dixon proved to be a matter of good fortune. Judge Dixon was quite influential. He could speak well. He made the real Highway Department contacts we needed and aroused interest and help. Still, progress was slow.

I have never forgotten one day, when the judge and I had been in Hyden, attending a Fiscal Court meeting. About "dusky dark" we started the ten mile horseback trip home to Wooton. Rain had poured down all day— and still was doing so. But we felt we must get home. As we came to the edge of North Fork, it was just light enough to see the surging river looking like an ocean tide "coming in." "Think we can make it?" asked the Judge. "Well, I've forded the river before in a tide," I answered. "Guess we can try."

It took a little persuasion to get the horses into the water, but they finally made the start. "I'll go first, you follow me. You know a horse does swim," the Judge said with a smile.

Grasping the bridle a bit tighter, I planted my feet more firmly in the stirrups and said, "I'll be okay." I started bravely to follow a path through the surging waters. Deeper, deeper we went, until I could feel the horse swimming. My ankles were swimming, too, deep in the tide! The water became deeper and deeper; it was almost to my hips. The Judge was talking, but I couldn't understand him. Finally, I could feel my Dixie being swept down the stream. He could no longer swim against the tide. "Well, this is it," I said, and with another prayer for help, and a furious tug at my bridle, I could feel a slight turn in our direction. I could faintly see that the Judge had reached the opposite bank and was motioning wildly to me. With yet another tug and a prayer, I felt we were at last coming out of the worst of the force of the tide. In a very few minutes, we joined the Judge and his horse, safe on the other side. We were suddenly aware that we had swum the entire width of the North Fork of the Kentucky River—on horseback!

Talking with "Mother Rose" one day, one of our men said, "Miss McCord, you don't really expect to have a pike way up here in these hills, do you?" "I most certainly do," she replied. "Do you expect me to be riding horseback the rest of my life?"

In the early Twenties, a resolution was passed by our Community League asking the Legislature to "authorize" a road from London, Kentucky, to Manchester, Hyden, Hindman and Big Sandy. The resolution, and Miss McCord's efforts and tenacity, brought Governor Fields to Wooton, accompanied by Major Helburn, a highway commissioner.

A great bunch of children walking with banners, flags, cheers, and songs, met the Governor's party, as they arrived on horseback on the last half mile of their journey. Such a day had never happened before in Leslie County! There was a big meeting and a wonderful community picnic dinner. As the day's festivities were about over, the Governor said, "If we don't build another foot of road anywhere in Kentucky this year, we will build this road in Leslie County!"

The voting date for a bond issue was set. Many folks said, "It's all impossible—this can't go through"; but, on the big day, and in spite of heavy rain, the bond issue *was* passed, 7 to 1! Our faithful horse Dixie carried many people up and down the creeks that voting day.

In one wagonload of voters who came, a grandmother said, "I don't expect to live to see this road, but I'm a votin' for it for my grandchildren; I have lots of 'em, and

I want the best for 'em." When Governor Fields was told this story later, he replied, "I wish there were more Kentuckians with such a spirit." The grandmother's faith did not go unrewarded, for she did live to see a portion of the highway completed.

Miss McCord's efforts and tenacity were paramount. On one meeting occasion in Frankfort, she was told she had five minutes to speak for the Hyden road. Under her beautiful lavender, pansy-trimmed hat, and with determination on her radiant face, she spoke her piece. The $5,000.00 was immediately voted . . . a thousand dollars for each minute of her appeal.

I recall being in Louisville with her another time when she said, "I need money for some errands and our return, but I don't have any identification with me." When we went, complete strangers, into a bank close by, she told the teller of her need to cash a check. "I know you don't know me, but you may call the minister of Fourth Avenue Church. I know Dr. Welsh."

The teller looked at her and said, "Miss McCord, anyone with a face like yours needs no other identification! How much do you need?"

The school picture at Wooton was little better than that of the roads at the beginning. Many times there had been no schools of any description; at other times only short term ones, beginning in July and running through December or January, depending on the severity of the winter. Children always had to wait until the crops were "laid by." Their help was needed in the cornfields—or so it always was assumed. Until now, the value of an education had not really been pondered, although parents did earnestly wish for a better life for their children.

Many activities aside from daily school were carried on at the little schoolhouse and helped to give it greater value. It was our one and only public building. Many times its capacity was so stretched we found ourselves having to meet out of doors.

So, we began talking of building a new "community

house," where the workers would live and where all community interests would center. With help from our Mission Board, considerable volunteer labor, and the gift of most materials—including lumber cut from the hills—our first community house was built. Although it was our home, it was the very center of all of our community activities . . . open to our people twenty-four hours a day.

Miss McCord felt that the heritage of mountain crafts should not be lost. She was very happy, therefore, when she found a teacher who could carry those on. Miss Minnie Klar became an important part of our small staff, teaching any who wanted to renew it the art of weaving, basketry, quilting, or anything in the sewing line. Another small building was secured and fixed over for her use. It became our Fireside Industry Cottage.

The small children and young folks at Wooton were given special opportunities in our church program through Christian Endeavor. Along with the Sunday School program, this interdenominational program was just for "the young." I think there never has been such a challenge for Christian training as Christian Endeavor offered. What a response we received from these mountain youngsters! There were groups for Juniors, Intermediates, and Seniors. These groups included intensive Bible study and followed any program a denomination wanted for its special church. The children learned to form their committees and were taught how to lead a meeting. Topics of the day were discussed and made a part of the weekly meetings.

How we worked. But what fun we had also. We found ourselves taking our place in meetings and conventions all over Kentucky! Through a generous friend of Miss McCord, passes were given to us on the L. & N. Railroad. These trips were the first adventures our mountain children had had into the "outside world," with its trains, cars, electricity and bathrooms. The excitement and joy was wonderful. We found we were quite like other people, and that they were quite like us. *"God hath made of one blood all nations."*

I remember especially one meeting we had in Ashland. Coming home that Sunday night—after we had been entertained in homes of the church people—I missed one of our little boys. Somewhat distraught, I said, "Let's go back to the church; he may be there." We retraced our steps, and sure enough, there was little Brunner on the steps. "I knowed you'd come back and get me," was his greeting, not a bit upset or terrified.

Our joy knew no bounds, and we could hardly contain ourselves when for two years we held the State Christian Endeavor Banner as the best Junior Christian Endeavor Society in all of Kentucky! "We're Juniors from Wooton, no livelier bunch can you find."

Our farms were very poor. They had been worked and worked through the years with no care or agricultural program of any sort. Was there, we wondered, a county agent? A home demonstration agent? Yes, we found that they existed and that they worked out of the University of Kentucky. But they had never been asked to come to Leslie County. In fact, they did not even seem to know that there was a Leslie County in Kentucky! Writing directly to the state and the University for help brought the answer: "Leslie is a pauper county. We have too many demands from counties who can pay their agents to consider your request from Leslie, which has no money." What an indictment from our own state officials! The hurt and discouragement of this harsh response almost brought tears.

But Miss McCord wrote back: "Don't tell me Leslie is a pauper county. No one knows this better than I. But we have *people* here; real, honest to goodness Americans who, along with other Kentuckians, deserve a chance—an opportunity, to learn and grow so they'll not continue to be paupers. Do you not feel a responsibility toward these Kentuckians who have such great needs? Aren't the mountains a part of Kentucky?"

The reply came: "You've got me. Get your fiscal court to appropriate $500.00; we'll do the rest."

With utter devotion and everlasting stick-to-itiveness, Miss McCord won once again.

County Home Demonstration Agents, with other "specialists" from the University, finally found us 'way back in our isolated hills. Their services helped ever so much to make Leslie County an "un-pauper" county. More than fifty years later now, this extension program is going strong. Leslie County has human resources richer than its ample ones of coal. And it was the church that had the vision to believe in these resources.

The Kentucky Department of Health was also contacted, and it too responded. Never before this had the mountains known any kind of help, medically, from the state. But soon state M.D.'s found their way to our hills, and clinics became an important part of our program. Kerosene lamps, lanterns, and flashlights "lighted the way." Water, carried by bucketfuls, was sterilized on a coal burning stove. No phones, no refrigeration, no electricity . . . but our clinics still took place!

Children arrived on horseback or on foot for tonsilectomies, or to see a "tooth dentist" who would take over so carefully and skillfully that there would be no air of emergency. The children would stay one night after an operation, sleeping on pallets on the floor. They would go home the next morning, when others would arrive to take their places.

We thanked the Great Physician for the skill and help of our Kentucky doctors and surgeons, who were fast becoming our good friends. Health education became a large part of our community program, with immunization—the very first in the county—in as many schools as we could reach. Of course, there was also bedside care, in times of sickness, and visiting in homes for the delivery of babies and for prenatal and postnatal care.

Little by little, hookworm, tapeworm, trachoma, rickets, t.b., and typhoid—all so prevalent and all so untouched before—were treated. Preventive programs were begun, and unsanitary conditions were improved.

In 1926 Mrs. Mary Breckinridge came to Hyden to head up what was to become the Frontier Nursing Service. Such a welcome addition were they, with their wonderful, expanding program of health, covering all of Leslie County. We were happy to provide their first orientation and to share our facilities when they began. Mary Rose McCord had cleared the path they were to follow.

One of our most active Wooton colleagues and a good friend was Gordon Redwine, who had "come over the ridge" from Virginia. As a man who disdained liquor, he acquired some bitter enemies. But he was deeply interested in helping the mountain folks and provided considerable care over the decade or more of his stay. His medical school studies had been left unfinished because of an angry encounter he had had with one of his professors. This mattered little as he served the mountain folk. A nice measure of his not resenting my arrival with "fotched on" ideas and standards was evident early in his having remarked to his wife, "I just met the prettiest little girl I ever saw. She's a nurse from Illinois, who's come to Wooton."

News of our clinics had gone rather far and wide. And this time, a letter had come to Miss McCord from a young man named Samuel VanderMeer, over in Breathitt County.

"I have heard of your clinics," he wrote. "I have some children here who need medical help. I can't get it here and wonder if I may bring three or four of them to your next clinic?"

"Of course," Miss McCord wrote back. "We can certainly make room for a few more children." She was always happy to reach out, thankful to help any mountain child, anywhere . . . Little did I know what *this* "reaching out" was going to mean!

The day before our next clinic, the young Mr. Vander-Meer arrived with his children. They had ridden horseback across some thirty miles of "creeks 'n hollers."

The Louisville doctors from the State Board of Health —and their supplies—had come by horseback for the final six miles of their journey. After welcoming them and finishing the hectic unloading of all "equipment," we all sat down to a hearty chicken dinner. Afterward we visited around the open fireplace. Then there was the "settling down" . . . finding a place for all to sleep. Somehow a corner was found for everyone, with beds fashioned on the floor for the children.

And the next day—another busy and wonderful clinic! Even in our primitive hospital, without electricity, running water, phone or bathroom, there was an air of efficient, skillful service. Our most critical needs were supplied by the doctors, who seemed to enjoy our challenging conditions.

Since the children were required to stay the night after their surgery, Mr. VanderMeer stayed, too, looking after his group. When all seemed finished and the young'uns had been "put to bed," we all decided 'twas time for a break and for making a batch of candy. (Even missionaries have a sweet tooth!) Our little group of "night nurses" had a good chance to visit, talking of the work in the hills and of opportunities and plans roundabout us.

Mr. VanderMeer said he was so glad to have this help for his children and that he'd like to bring others from Morris Fork for another clinic, since they didn't have anything over there.

"Morris Fork," I asked, "where is that?" "Just a little spot in Breathitt County," he replied, "about six miles from Buckhorn. That's where Mr. Murdoch is starting a school and I've been helping him. He sent me to Morris Fork to see what I could do there. I started a little Sunday School and am visiting with the folks—they don't seem to have much."

Several months later, it was time for another clinic. Sure enough, back he came. Then, even if there were no clinic, he'd appear. It didn't take Wooton Creekers long to notice the rather frequent visits of this "young boy preacher from Breathitt." Since we had a Florence Reist, a "brought on" teacher whose name was pronounced "Rice," someone said, "I wonder if it's going to be Pease or Rice?"

"I read in the Bible one time," Sam told some Lees College interviewers many years later, "that it's not good for a man to live alone, and I decided if the Bible said that, I'd better be doing something right. Of course, there wasn't anything else to marry but a woman, and one day my travels took me over to Leslie County and I was introduced to this young nurse, Nola Pease.

"We looked at each other and we got to talking; then we made the mistake of walking down to the post office together and some lady saw us. She had a dream that night that this young man, who rode in on horseback, and this nurse, were going to get married. We hardly knew each other, but we'd heard about the dream and rather than have that woman go through life not believing in dreams, my wife proposed to me. But we liked to do a bit of courting before we got married, and it was a 35-mile horseback trip from where I lived to where she lived. I had to ford the Kentucky River twice, right where the lodge [Buckhorn Lake State Park] is now, and cross two mountains, go through a place called 'Hell for Certain' in order to get to Wooton's Creek near the mouth of the Cutshin."

Sam used to like to tell everyone "John Fox wrote about *Courtin on Cutshin,* but I did it."

During one of his visits, he reminded us of the very first clinic, when the children were getting ready for the horseback trip back home the next day. The doctor had said, "These children are fine. Just let them ride home slowly, and do not let them get wet. In case of rain, you must get them under cover." But about ten miles from Morris Fork, black clouds appeared, along with thunder and lightning. With no buildings in sight for shelter, Sam gathered the children and their horses around him and said, "Let's pray—the doctor said you couldn't get wet." So, bowing their heads, they asked for special care. Then, while sheltered under a tree, the rain came down in torrents all around them. As the rain ceased, and they rode out, "dry shod," Sam said, "Let's pray again." They thanked God for His special care, and as they splashed through the creeks the rest of the way home, they sang cheerfully.

Wedding plans were soon in the air. The big day was set—June 9! There was much excitement . . . and some consternation.

"We'll have a big dinner," the mothers said; "We'll ask everybody to come."

Since there was no church, a garden ceremony was planned. As we talked of bridesmaids, ushers, flower girls . . . everyone wondered what such talk was all about.

But Sam and I had much to talk about also. "I'm sorry, I don't feel I can move to Wooton," he said. "I just can't leave Morris Fork. I hope you'll see just how badly you're needed there too," he added, looking earnestly at me.

"There are Frontier Nurses and other workers here at Wooton. There is no one at Morris Fork. They just have nothing. I thought I was going to South America, but after I'd had my last meeting in the little schoolhouse, which was so crowded with people that some had to stay out-doors, a man said, 'You think you are going away. You may go for a little bit, but we're goin to pray you back!' And they've done just that. I feel I must stay here. We can make a second Wooton's Creek at Morris Fork."

Sam was very persuasive, but it was difficult to think about leaving. There were some sleepless nights and many prayers. Finally I comforted myself, I wasn't leaving the mountains, I was just "reaching out." Talking with Miss McCord, the decision was made. It was to be Morris Fork! Then, I wondered, could I do it? Leave Wooton, my boys and girls—my babies I'd brought into the world—my wonderful friends, all I loved there? With the Frontier Nursing Service getting settled and road improvements really on the way, all was not as bleak as it had seemed when I had arrived ten years before. Life and work at the community house would go on!

I wanted very much to take Sam to Illinois to meet my family at Thanksgiving time. Since there were some extra folks around to carry on, Miss McCord said we should go ahead.

Soon after our happy arrival in Allendale, an occasion arose for my father to introduce Sam. "This is my future son-in-law, Mr. . . . er . . . " He turned to Sam saying, "What did you say your name was?"

Sam bore no hard "feelins." He knew that a Dutch name like VanderMeer wasn't easy to remember. But folks liked and accepted him as much as if his name had been . . . Pease. We stayed about a week in Allendale. He helped in the service on Sunday and went visiting folks with his father-in-law-to-be.

The next spring, wedding plans proceeded swiftly. Reverend Samuel McKee, a pastor in Hyden, was asked to officiate for us. He and Sam were very good friends. They had become known as "First and Second Samuel." I had six little namesakes who wanted to be flower girls. My Sunday School class of young people would be ushers and bridesmaids, and two others of "my babies" ring bearers. We even planned to move the foot treadle organ out on the grass for the wedding march. All Leslie County would be invited . . . and my family would come from Illinois!

Sam made his horseback visits as frequently as he could. The date came closer and closer. It seemed that all was about "wrapped up" and ready. But about a week before the 9th, the weather became very sultry and unusually hot. Each day brought more clouds, and on the night of June 7, the rain began. It lasted all through the night, and the next day. It came in torrents. Creek beds quickly overflowed, and an honest-to-goodness flood was upon us. Only those who have been in the mountains and lived through a "flash flood" know what that means. Harder and harder the rains came, and by the morning of the 9th everything around us was under water! Fortunately, we were on a high hill, safe from the water that surrounded us and that changed the grounds into a lake. Such a flood I had never seen!

Alas for our garden wedding! What could we do? Absolutely nothing! There was no telephone, no chance to get a message to or from Sam. No chance to even get a message to the railroad station, where it could get out. Just no way to do anything but wait until the rain stopped and the waters receded. Even our horse or muleback travel was impossible over the flooded creeks. We thanked God that our lives were spared, and we just waited.

In a couple of days, our world began to dry out, and roads were passable again. Sam appeared, and the 14th was chosen as our new wedding date. I learned later that one of my classmates from Blessing Hospital had come to Typo on the train the morning of the 9th and had sat in the little station, all day, waiting for the night train!

I had sent most of my personal clothing to a cleaners in Lexington. Word came from the Post Office in Hazard that it had come, but was under water there. All my clothes to begin life with at Morris Fork! Fortunately, I had my wedding dress at Wooton.

I had wondered earlier how I was to get a wedding dress, with practically no income. The answer came from St. Clair, Michigan. When I was a baby there, my mother was a very good friend of the Moore family, who owned the Diamond Crystal Salt Company. They had a young daughter, Harriet, who became very fond of this young baby at the manse. All through the years, even when we moved, my mother kept in contact with the Moores. I kept in touch with Harriet, and one time she visited me at Wooton. Then came her wonderful wedding gift to me . . . one hundred dollars! Such wealth I'd never heard of, but here was my wedding dress. I was also able to buy material for dresses for my bridesmaids and little flower girls. Such fun we had making these—with the help of all my Wooton mothers.

June 14th arrived . . . a beautiful and glorious day! All

Our wedding portrait.

flooded debris had been cleared away and the garden was lovely again. We needed no special decorations for the lovely, outdoor setting. We did rope off a garden path with colored crepe paper, where the children were to march, and we had several rehearsals. The little "Nolas" were radiant in their rainbow dresses. The strains of the Wedding March on the pump organ drifted over the hillsides of those Cumberland Mountains for the very first time! One of the flower girls said, "We packed the bail"—(carried the veil!)

After the chicken dinner, which all the folks of Wooton prepared and enjoyed, there were games on the lawn—seemed no one wanted to go home. Folks did begin to leave late in the day, and by six o'clock, we were ready to climb the hill to our honeymoon cottage. We were to stay there for a couple of days. But, with odds 'n ends left to do around the community house, we lingered another hour.

Suddenly such noise you never heard! A real, honest-to-goodness "shivaree" began. Poundings on cans, kettles, anything in sight! The young people had come back to pay a call. Sam was put astride the proverbial "board," to be taken and dumped in the creek. But they decided only to "ride" him instead. He was pumped up and down the hill—all over the yard. We had been slightly prepared for this, and so began passing out candy and lemonade, hoping 'twould all end soon. By ten o'clock, they finally drifted away.

Happily, but a bit wearily, we climbed up the hill to our cottage. Sitting down, and heaving a deep breath, I said, "Sam, I don't believe this is over. I have a feelin' they'll be back. Any candy left?" Just about that time the music did indeed begin all over! They banged around out-doors until we asked them to come into the cottage, where there was a bit more candy. So, we had another party, with more fun, this time until midnight. Finally I said, "Now, you have to go home—we must get some rest, and you, too." Reluctantly, they said goodnight . . . and this time, didn't come back. We blew out our kerosene light at last.

It must have been about 1:00 a.m., when the familiar call came, "Hello, hello! Is Miss Nola there? We need her!"

Unbelievingly, I jumped up, ran to the door, saying, "I'm just married and am not going out anymore. I can't go tonight. You'll have to get one of the Frontier nurses."

"They might have known I couldn't come tonight," I said to Sam . . . a bit guiltily.

We had about an hour's sleep when the call was repeated. Again, struggling to the door, I said, "You'll have to take your wife to Hyden or get a nurse from there. I can't go. I don't have any of my things here."

Then I really did feel guilty. It was the first time since coming to Wooton that I had refused a call. But the guilty feeling didn't last long. Within the hour, the voice called out again, "Miss Pease, you'll have to come. We have a nurse from Hyden, but she's afraid there is going to be trouble. She doesn't know what to do. Please come and help her!" Then he handed me a note from the nurse, giving the same message. I just couldn't refuse the third time! Quickly, Sam jumped out of bed. We threw on some clothes and were off. Fortunately, the cabin was close enough so that we were able to walk. In a couple of hours our baby arrived—no complications.

How Sam loved to tell folks in the years that followed that we had a baby on our wedding night!

Word had come from Sam's family in Paterson. "Even though we couldn't get to the wedding, we want to see the bride and bridegroom real soon." Along with the eager invitation came a gift of money for our transportation.

We hadn't really planned for such a big journey, but we did want the folks back there to be part of our happy event. And I wanted so much to meet them. So off we went, on a New Jersey "honeymoon."

Sam had of course done the unthinkable; he had married a girl who wasn't Dutch! I wasn't too sure how I'd be received—an Un-Dutch stranger in a Dutch house, al-

50

Four of my namesake babies . . . and flower girls: (left to right) Nola Smith, Nola Hoskins, Nola Baker and Nola Joseph—June 14, 1927.

though I had some sense that anything Sam did was just fine. He was the idol of the household.

After the thirteen mile horseback ride to Typo and the L. & N. connection to Lexington, we began our long ride on the "George Washington," the special C. & O. train that made a daily trip to Washington and New York. What a quiet and relaxing time this was—after our hectic wedding activities. What an extra special treat going to the diner, with nary a care in the world.

In Paterson we were received royally. I was taken right in with no chance to feel like a stranger.

There were eleven children in Sam's family. All nine who were alive were part of our welcome. I was sorry of course—as Sam was—that his father and mother could not have lived to enjoy our special time. But a host of brothers, sisters, cousins, aunts, and uncles initiated me

4

Mary Rose McCord

Tardy Tribute
to a Great Lady

I am come that they might have life, and that they might have it more abundantly.

—John 10.10

*   *   *

The abiding gifts of Mary Rose McCord to the people of the Kentucky mountains have not been acknowledged adequately by those of us who had the wonderful privilege of knowing her and working alongside her. I hope that I may have compensated for this in some small way here.

When Sam and I set out from Wooton to begin the first of what would be our many years at Morris Fork, we were beneficiaries as well as friends of "Mother Rose." For a decade—an entire second schooling in my life—she had shown me a living definition of what it meant to pursue a more abundant life for those she came to love and serve. She had shown me and, from time to time, Sam, how to be strong and steadfast in believing that, with God's help, such a life could be achieved. Even when resources were meager and obstacles were across our path, she remained tenacious and radiant; and through it all, she infused the importance of a sense of humor. I smile now when I recall the time our very young Billy was told to call her "Gramma Rose." Billy became quizzical and asked,

53

Mary Rose McCord

"Where's Grampa Rose?" "That's what I'd like to know," she answered.

What we set out to do at Morris Fork, "Mother Rose" had already begun or completed at Wooton—with her concern for community health, recreation, better conditions of daily living, schools, and worship of a living and loving God. We went forth as her students, as well as her friends. She had shown us the way, and so she is a special part of this story.

In commemorating Miss McCord's decision to go to Wooton's Creek in 1917, and her achievement that followed it, her Berea friend and occasional comrade-in-arms, Mary Dupuy, wrote, " . . . pioneer blood is rich and Miss McCord was a rare combination of home-lover and adventurer. She asked for a rest and then a quest. The quest was to go farther into the mountains to find a community —it must, she said, be in Kentucky—that yearned for, yet was not supplied with, more than crumbs from life's abundant table. The Board of National Missions assured support, and she spent a year prospecting for the location of her choice. In Hyden, a settlement in Leslie County, one of the inner and isolated counties of Kentucky, a Presbyterian minister bespoke her attention on behalf of his county, untouched by any form of modern communication or contact. For a week, 'The Lord's Prospector,' as she was once lovingly called, rode horseback up and down and across the streams, across the ridges and into the hollows, in the hottest September in history, searching out the inaccessible, mountain-bound localities. At once her interest was caught by the Wooton Creek neighborhood on Cutshin. She rode miles to other settlements that had already begun their work. At Pine Mountain, William Creech advised, 'Go back to Cutshin—they want me and Katherine and Ethel (Miss Pettit and Mrs. Zande) to go but we have more than we can do here. Go to the mouth of 'Ooton's Creek on Cutshin.' It was there that she did go, where 'a flock was waiting for a shepherd.' A meeting was arranged in the ill-lighted schoolhouse with many men and women of Wooton's Creek and a small group from New York, and the situation and its possibilities talked through. On Wooton's Creek, in Leslie County, self- styled at that time 'the lostest county in Kentucky,' the quest was ended. It is here that Miss McCord was most closely identified and her major life work began.''

At Wooton, Miss McCord met, with vigor and grace, what she herself described so well as "the Challenge of the Mountains," in an article that appeared in *The Home Mission Monthly* in January of 1920. Because there is an eloquence to it that would be disturbed by any extraction of a phrase here, or a paragraph there, I want to include all of it here. As I read through it again, after fishing it from the archives of the Presbyterian Historical Society in Philadelphia, I could hear her voice so clearly.

The Church of Christ is today face to face with the greatest challenge which ever confronted her—that of using the spirit of service and sacrifice which so dominated people during the war in the greater warfare of taking the world for Christ. The demand of the day is for trained leadership. Every rural community feels this and especially is it true of the more isolated districts. On this need we base our claim that the mountains of the Southland offer to the Church today the greatest, most compelling challenge—a call for help to help themselves toward the highest and best development. A man who desires to make an investment seeks one that will bring the largest returns; one who wishes to make a gift usually remembers first his own family. These principles applied to the church would bring large sums to the mountains, for here, in these young people, are found those who, if given an opportunity for Christian education, would furnish recruits for the ministry and the mission fields and leaders in all lines of work; here are found members of the family who because of isolation have been 'left out' of many opportunities for development which

have come to other communities. What better invest-
ment, what greater incentive for giving, can the
Church ask?

Beautiful for situation, these sections traversed by
the Appalachian mountains are destined to become the
richest parts of the states. Great resources of mineral
and coal are here as yet largely undeveloped; opportu-
nities in fruit growing, animal husbandry, poultry, and
the like, as yet undiscovered; greatest of all the large
numbers of 'little Americans' waiting their chance for
an education.

Development along all these lines is surely coming.
Since this is true why comes the challenge with peculiar
force to the Church? Why need she bestir herself? One
need only to visit any community where the railroad
and mining camps have already entered to find the
answer. 'An ounce of prevention is worth a pound of
cure.'

The call then is to the Church to get on to a com-
munity regeneration through the developing of Chris-
tian leaders from among the people—a work of coop-
eration, of doing with, not for, the people. If, my
reader, you have seen, as I have, one-mule teams try-
ing to drag a heavy load over a mountain road, you
would realize how well nigh impossible a task it seems;
hitch another mule to the load and it moves more easi-
ly; if yet another is hitched on in front, how much
more quickly the load travels, albeit the same obstacles
are in the way. Cannot this three-mule team fitly repre-
sent the community, the state, and the Church, with
the latter in the lead?

The needs are many. The people, willing to do all
they can, desire the best for their children. Shall we
deny and hear not the call? More constructive preach-
ing is needed; strong men, the best the Church can fur-
nish; Christian teachers, trained to teach, are needed;
men who can minister to the whole man, translating
the Gospel of Jesus Christ by an all-round service,
preaching the Word, interesting himself in better

57

roads, better agriculture, better homes, better schools, better churches. Money is needed; money to supplement the funds available from the community and the state to build schoolhouses worthy the name and to make the school more nearly such as city children have had these many years; money to build churches, community churches, is sadly needed. A well equipped schoolhouse and a church in every community center where children can get a proper training, where all people may worship and find a place of service in the name of Him who prayed that we 'might all be one;' is this too much to ask of those who all their lives have had these blessings?

These are some of the opportunities awaiting the Church in the Southern mountains. The challenge is here. God grant that the Church may straightway hear and answer with workers and money, "here am I."

In the marvelous person of Mary Rose McCord, the Church answered eloquently.

It answered also with the work and person of Helen Dingman. Sam and I knew Helen during most of our mountain years. She had come from New York, initially as a representative of our Board of Home Missions. Then, around 1925, she returned to work as a missionary at Smith, a small community in Harlan County.

Helen and Miss McCord visited one another as often as horse or mule trips could be taken, to talk of challenges and opportunities and to share ideas and plans . . . She joined the Berea College faculty after several years of inspired mountain service, and remained very active until her death in 1978.

No one better stated the Christian call under which Miss McCord and those of us who followed her worked than Helen Dingman did in an address she gave in Des Moines in 1922.

When Jesus said: "I am come that they might have life, and that they might have it more abundantly," it seems to me that He wanted that evangelistic message worked out in every department of our lives, and in our community program we try to make Christianity the dynamic in every phase of our community life. But community leaders should not go in to do the work themselves, but with the purpose of helping the people to help themselves. We have no right to take away their natural heritage of initiative and leadership. It is the slowest method and ofttimes very discouraging, but unless our program is constructive it would be better to stay out altogether. Nor should we go into a community with any set program of accomplishment that may have fitted in some other section. We must first have the art of being neighbors, study this situation and be ready for the "open doors" of opportunity.

All of us who came into the mountains to find meaning for our lives and the lives we found there could take encouragement and inspiration from the kind of "neighboring" Miss McCord had done. She had not only followed the suggestion of William Creech to "go back to Cutshin," she had also heeded his own hope for the children of the Kentucky mountains. Creech had said:

I don't look after wealth for them . . . I look after the prosperity of our nation. I want all younguns taught to serve the livin' God. Of course, they won't do that, but they can have good and evil laid before them and they can choose which they will. I have heart and cravin' that our people may grow better.

"Do you think I am happy in Kentucky?" Sam wrote on the back of this snapshot for his brother Jacob.

5

Preparing for "South America"

Sam's Eastern Boyhood

*And Samuel said unto the people, Fear not:
ye have done all this wickedness: yet turn not
aside from following the Lord, but serve the
Lord with all your heart;*

*And turn ye not aside: for then should ye go
after vain things, which cannot profit nor
deliver; for they are vain.*

*For the Lord will not forsake his people for
his great name's sake: because it hath pleased
the Lord to make you his people.*

*Moreover as for me, God forbid that I
should sin against the Lord in ceasing to pray
for you: but I will teach the good and the right
way:*

*Only fear the Lord, and serve him in truth
with all your heart: for consider how great
things he hath done for you.*

I Samuel 12: 20-24

*   *   *

When Sam's brother "Jake" asked Eddie Ackerman
in 1978 about some of his boyhood memories, Eddie re-
called that both he and Sam had lived on North Tenth
Street in Prospect Park, New Jersey. "It was a dead-end

61

street . . . only nine houses on it. This was in the horse and buggy days . . . We looked up to Sammy VanderMeer as king of us kids. He was kind and had a heart of gold.

"In the summertime, after supper, all of us kids and our leader would play all kinds of games in the street and when it almost got dark Sammy would say it was time to go in . . .

"In our early days, if any of us kids was to start grammar school, Sammy would take us.

"Sammy and I, we both liked to have a garden, but I did not have room in my yard. So he gave me a space in his.

"We had many a good time together."

In the VanderMeer family, no one seems to remember Sam more vividly than his nephew, Lambert. He still savors some of his boyhood memories of Sam's teenage years around Paterson.

"Sam, and my dad and I, went fishing in the Morris Canal. I just couldn't seem to get a bite. Well, Sam found a dead fish close by. He dove in and without my being aware of it put the fish on my bent safety pin hook. My dad said he thought I had a bite. But when I pulled up my line and took the surprise fish off my hook, I said, 'It sound like a dead one.'

" . . . While Sam was staying with us in Little Falls, he would place a little something he had made or found under my pillow every night. Sometimes it was just a penny. I've had a lot of fun keeping up that tradition with my own youngsters.

" . . . My dad was a painter in those years, and he considered times to be good if he made a dollar and a half a day. One time he gave Sam four whole dollars to go out and get an old pair of his own shoes repaired. Well, Sam came back home with his shoes unrepaired. He tried to offer some explanation but finally confessed that he had given the four dollars to a Dutch family with five youngsters who seemed to have some real needs. Sam kept on

62

cutting cardboard to put inside his own shoes with holes in their soles.

" . . . Sam was a real good sport. I can remember having Mart VanderMeer over to stay with us once when Sam was a part of the household. The three of us would get a whip stick about three feet long, put a crabapple on the end and see who could whip it the longest distance. It was good fun, but Sam made it even more fun by really making a game out of it.

"Sam never told me to do anything. He always asked me, and for some reason I'd go and do it. He had a way about him and people just couldn't say 'No.'"

Until I began to search out and remember the fixins of this small book, I had not really heard these or, for that matter, very many other recollections of that Dutch boy who would go into the Kentucky mountains. My but how well they reveal my Sam, whom ever so many folks came to know and love.

As I sorted painfully through Sam's things, after the Lord had taken him, I came upon several penciled yellow sheets clipped together. In some quiet corner and moment, he had written them. They were really the first pages of this book.

The last of these handwritten sheets tell of his first weeks in the mountains. They have the very sound of his voice in them. Followed by a few excerpts I have taken from letters he sent back that summer of '23 to his teachers and friends at the Union Missionary Training Institute in Brooklyn, New York, and at the Star of Hope Mission in Paterson, New Jersey, they reveal his glowing human light—a light that had already illumined the path we would follow together at Morris Fork . . .

Owsley County has been the birthplace of many outstanding Kentuckians. One of the greatest of these was the Rev. Isaac H. Gabbard, who in his lifetime led more people to Jesus Christ than any other mountain preacher. "Brother Ike," as he was affectionately called, was always ready to ride his horse wherever his services were needed. One of his "preaching points" was at the Junior Hall at the mouth of the Burton Fork of Longs Creek. When Brother Ike came, folks travelled for miles to hear this man of God. Many times his meetings were interrupted by the yells of drunken men and the roar of guns.

As Brother Ike would ride his horse back to his home on Cow Creek, his heart would be troubled about the children growing up in such an environment and he would pray that God would send someone to teach the children and help make the area a better place. Little did he realize that in Prospect Park, New Jersey, there was a young man who had just been converted and was seeking God's will for his life. The young man did not know about Brother Ike's burden of prayer, but God, who works in mysterious ways, was aware of both supplicants, and in His own way brought the two together. The person whom God used to bring about the meeting of these two men was Mrs. Elizabeth Blackman, a member of the Lafayette Avenue Presbyterian Church in Brooklyn, N. Y.

"Granny" Blackman had conducted a mission in Brooklyn which was under the auspices of her church, and the young Sam VanderMeer, who was seeking God's will for his life, became her assistant. When she left her work in Brooklyn, she came to Buckhorn, where Dr. Harvey Murdoch had established a church and school which was supported by the Lafayette Avenue Church. Several months later, she invited her young assistant to come to Kentucky for a summer vacation. In June 1923, this young man, who was to spend almost fifty years of his life in the mountains, made his first trip into Kentucky. After he had been there several months, he and Brother Ike met; after a brief visit, Brother Ike reached out his hand and said—"I believe you are the answer to my prayers."

Before coming to the Kentucky Mountains, I had read many articles about the area and its people. Some of the information was most disturbing, and friends tried to persuade me to serve the Lord in another part of the world. Upon reaching Lexington, where it was necessary to wait for the L. & N. RR. train which left for the mountains about midnight, I began to wonder whether I should have taken the advice of my friends. While thinking about this, I heard someone whistling in the station. It was a little newsboy and he was whistling "Be not dismayed what 'er betide, God will take care of you. All you may need He will provide, God will take care of you." I thanked God for the message; all through the years the truth of that song has been realized.

The first summer was spent at Buckhorn, where Witherspoon College was located. During the week, we hoed corn in the bottoms and on the hillsides, and the weekends were spent in conducting services at Buckhorn, Boonington and Squabble Creek. Since there were no roads all our travel was on horseback. I had planned to spend the summer in Kentucky and then go on to South America where I felt God was calling. When school opened in the fall, Mr. Murdoch asked me to teach in the fourth grade. Later he requested my help in teaching at Cow Creek until another teacher could be secured.

One hot Sunday afternoon, young Ben Miller and I rode a mile from Perry County—through Breathitt—and into Owsley County. It had been arranged that I would preach at the Cow Creek schoolhouse at two o'clock and then make my home with Uncle Dan Callahan and his wife during my stay in that community. When we reached Uncle Dan's house, we found that he was not at home, but his wife was sitting on the porch. I told her that Mr. Murdoch had said I could board there. She looked me over and decided against it. I then asked her permission to leave my belongings on her porch until after the meeting. When she gave her consent, I emptied my belongings out of the saddle-pockets and sent Ben back to Buckhorn with

Sam and "Granny" (Elizabeth) Blackman, who inspired him in Brooklyn to join her for a summer's work in the mountains.

the mule. I found a good sized crowd at the schoolhouse, and they listened attentively to the new 'furrin' preacher. After the service, I was asked where I was going to stay and I had to tell them that I didn't have any idea where I would stay. Then an old man approached me and told me I could stay at his house. I accepted his invitation and we soon arrived at the house where I had left my belongings. To my dismay, he told me that this was his house! The little old lady was still sitting on the porch, and I began to wonder who was boss. This matter was soon decided when he told his wife that I would be staying there. She did not look very happy about it, and when suppertime came she simply uncovered the remains of the noon meal. I found it difficult to eat the cold sweet potatoes, gravy and other foods. After supper the old folks went to bed and I was left alone on the porch of their cabin. I was feeling lonely and sorry for myself when suddenly the stillness was broken by the call of the whippoorwill. It was so insistent and sustained. Then I heard the sound of hoofbeats and looked and saw a man on horseback approaching. He stopped, hitched his horse, came up on the porch and introduced himself as Pleas Turner, the principal of the school. He informed me that school began at eight—that I would have about twenty pupils and teach five subjects, one of which I had never studied. He further informed me that I should be able to find some textbook lying around in the school building. After he left, I felt considerably worse and woefully inadequate. I began to wonder why I hadn't listened to my friends who tried to discourage me from going to the mountains. Then out of the silence I seemed to hear a voice asking me whether I was in the mountains by choice or whether I believed God had called me. Being assured that it was the latter, there came to mind the beautiful 23rd Psalm. *"The Lord is my Shepherd, I shall not want."* All of a sudden I realized that because the Lord was my Shepherd I would not want for wisdom, guidance, or even acceptance in Uncle Dan's home. Fully assured that God had spoken, I retired and was soon asleep.

The next morning, Mrs. Callahan's attitude had changed. She had prepared a wonderful breakfast, and my own mother could not have been more thoughtful and attentive to my needs. I stayed at Cow Creek for one month and found that God can supply our needs when they are in the path of service. I told someone that I studied as hard as if it all depended on me, and then prayed as hard as if it all depended upon God.

Sam wrote with a special enthusiasm to those who had inspired him at the Missionary Training Institute:

How I wish you could be here on this porch with me to enjoy the beautiful scenery here in the Kentucky Mountains. It doesn't surprise me that the people who live here love their country in spite of the many drawbacks. There is something about these hills and mountains that seems to make one love them. How I do praise God for sending me here to witness for Him, and also to see the beauty of His handiwork. Isn't it a wonderful comfort to know that our precious Lord and Master is the Creator of these great mountains? How strong He is and how can we ever doubt Him when we see His work displayed on every hand!

I have been wanting to tell you for some time how much my training at the Union Missionary Training Institute has meant to me. God alone knows how grateful I am to Him for sending me there, and for laying it upon your heart to carry on the great work so faithfully . . . There are so many students today who leave their schools and colleges with a shattered faith, a torn up Bible, and nothing to offer the sin-sick souls to whom they are to minister. But praise God, no such thing happens to any student who comes to the National Bible Institute Schools! . . . My Bible is not a torn up book, full of doubtful passages, foolish stories and impossible miracles. My Bible to me is the living Word of God, inspired from cover to cover, and I'm so glad that now I have a working knowledge of it . . . The teachers . . . have meant so much to me. Each one a consecrated Christian, interested in the students as individuals . . .

. . . I had a very pleasant trip coming here, stopping at Philadelphia and Washington, D.C. When I reached Altro, Ky. I was met at the station by a boy with a horse which he told me I was to ride. I had never ridden before, but I got on and rode after my little guide. It was certainly a new experience for me. We traveled eight miles over the roughest country one can imagine; through creeks, over boulders, stumps, up and down mountain sides and in fact everything rough you can imagine. I received a warm welcome at Buckhorn and this made up for the rough journey.

My first month was a very busy one, farming, painting, building, preaching, teaching, gardening, haying, whitewashing, etc., etc. . . . I teach Bible and Writing in the Sixth Grade, and also do some substitute work in other grades. I am taking a few studies as

I have enough time to do some studying. I am taking Algebra, Second Year Latin, American Literature and Agriculture. On Sundays I mount my mule and go preaching in some of the schoolhouses along the creeks. I am getting much valued experience, and at the same time I hope I may be used to win some of these precious souls . . .

Sincerely yours in His service,

Samuel VanderMeer

In his letter to the Star of Hope Mission, back home in Paterson, Sam shared more of the same excitement that was in his letter to his teachers and schoolmates.

I do praise God for opening the way for me to come here. I have been here two months now and never once have I been sorry that I came . . . I have had many experiences since coming here, most of them pleasant. The mountaineers are such good, big-hearted people that one cannot help but love them. They are very hospitable and one never needs worry about a place to sleep or eat if he chances to be near a home.

How I wish you could go with me some Sunday to hold services. Little did I think about ten years ago when I went to church on Sundays, all dressed up, with two pennies and two peppermints in my pocket and a little Dutch cologne on my handkerchief, that some day I would be going to hold service myself in these mountains, traveling on a mule. A few Sundays ago I preached in Buckhorn in the morning, led Christian Endeavor in the afternoon and then mounted my mule and started out to help in a service up the creek. I had about three miles to travel, most of the distance through the creek itself. At times the water went over my shoes. I felt that I was soaked to my knees. I felt that I was a pretty sorry looking sight to help lead in a service but I had on a nice clean shirt and I was sure it would save the day—but alas, going down a hill, my mule's foot got caught and down she went, and of course I went right over her head and landed on the road with my clean white shirt. Well, I can assure you that it wasn't clean any longer, but I went to the service anyhow. My part was to teach a Sunday School class. I wish you could have been there. We found a nice place to sit in the woods, using stumps, rails, stones, etc. for seats. There were about thirty boys and girls present and oh, how they listened as I told them the blessed Gospel Story! I used the big, dirty mud stains on the front of my white shirt as an illustration, so you see it was alright after all.

The county I am in is considered to be the worst in Kentucky. The worst we have to fight is moonshine. Oh, if you only knew of the misery it has caused in this beautiful country! We hear shooting quite frequently and several have been shot and killed since I have come here. It is especially sad to see so many stalwart young men being ruined by this awful stuff—some call it Honey dew, White lightning, Honey from the rock, and Devil's soup. I believe the last is the most fitting name.

Morris Fork
1927-1969

Sunday school portrait—Morris Fork. 1928

6

The Early Years

SOME BACKGROUND PATCHES

Settlin'

According to Sigel Turner, the early settlers of what became Morris Fork had been on the side of the British during the Revolutionary War and had moved on westward after its outcome. They had started out for Kentucky from Mulberry Ford in North Carolina and, many ridges later, had brought their trek to an end in the area of Long's Creek and Riley's Fork.

The area came to know quite early a goodly number of Spicers, Haddixes, Stampers, Turners, Rileys and Morrises. The Rileys apparently spread themselves as far as the edges of the Bluegrass region, just south of Lexington.

The sharp contrast between Lexington and Morris Fork—a mere hundred miles away—was evident, even as early as the 1820's. By that decade, Lexington had become a small but growing city with many artists, physicians, clergymen, scientists and architects. It was the educational training ground of seventeen congressmen, six U.S. Senators, three governors and the President-to-be of the Confederacy. During 1817, Lexington had heard the very first performance of a Beethoven symphony anywhere in the United States!

While architects were designing homes for grace and elegance in the Bluegrass, John Morris' father bought the hollow in which he was to live for an old hog rifle. John himself once summed up for David Rule what those early days were like . . . "They raised what they lived on and lived on what they raised." Along with George Stamper, he could recall how the only clothes around had been made from woven yarn and how the moccasins were fashioned from "whang," home-tanned leather.

Lyla Cornett raised sheep, and the wool was sent away to be carded. When it came back, it was woven by her into suits for her little boys. It was very common for folks to have handmade woolen socks. Those who had no sheep and could do no weaving used grain sacks for bedding and underclothing. This was in a time when they were able to get grain in heavy, cotton "feed sacks," not burlap. Bedding was also "homemade"—the lovely quilts, blankets and coverlets—even the hand-woven sheets.

For many years, what came to be known as Morris Fork, had been known as Riley's Fork. How much the shift of a family or two, or something else, had to do with the change is uncertain. Morris Fork it became . . . and Morris Fork it is.

Talkin' and Preachin'

Our mountain folks spoke better and more interesting language than they have been depicted as speaking.

Coming to Appalachia from England, Ireland and Scotland, their forbears brought much of their old world heritage with them, especially in their speech. A good deal of their Chaucerian English has stuck through the years and is still in widespread use. It is rich and warm language, and it was music in our lives at Morris Fork.

A girl described her watch as being "strict," meaning it measured up to requirements of excellence. I "holped" my neighbor. I found a "waspers nestie." "I ain't beholden to ary a man." "Hit's a right smart child." "He's got a heap o' learnin." "Here's a poke full o' vegetables." "Am proud to see you." "Set a spell." "We love to have guesties take a night." These are all heard.

If one asks another to do something special, the answer, "I don't care if I do," really means he's delighted to oblige. A good thinker is "thoughty." A "fireboard" is a mantle over the fireplace. A new baby "favors his kin folks." A stranger, not born in the mountains, is "fotched on." A "well turned" person is one who gets on well with the neighbors. A well-known, and well-liked missionary was "the best fotched on, artificial man I ever saw."

"Would it be too much of a shockment if I stopped by?" was an inquiry made by a man who wanted to call on his neighbor after he had just shot someone.

Describing how she had seen someone pass, Mary Thompson said, "I throwed my eyes out o' the window and saw her go by."

At the end of the harvest season, crops are "laid by." "I feel no umbrage toward you" means I hold no grudge. And "I'm just bilin over with pure satisfaction," well, this speaks for itself better than any other words could!

Soon after Sam and I settled in at Morris Fork, we were told of a local mountain minister, Ike Gabbard, who had done much "circuit riding preaching" through the mountains, especially in the Morris Fork area. A man of very limited education, he had a great love for his Lord and a sense of burden for the mountain folk. As he would ride up and down Morris Fork Creek, fully aware of all the moonshining, shootings and feuds, his continual prayer was: "O Lord, please send us someone to come to help, to teach these people about Thee, and a better way of life." This was the burden of his soul. Very soon after coming to Morris Fork, Sam met Mr. Gabbard. Though a perfect stranger, Ike threw his arms around him, saying "You are the answer to my prayer! The Lord sent you here. God bless us as we work together for him." This was the beginning of a most beautiful friendship, and they drew closer and closer as, together, they preached and talked.

Well do I remember the first time I met Brother Ike Gabbard. It was after a Morris Fork church service. Sam and others had told me of his presence. But I was not prepared to meet such a person. The keenest of eyes, a look of half smile, half defiance—and a handshake that seemed to grip your whole being. Even in his advanced years, he continued his miles of horseback riding and preaching. Many times he would attend Presbytery or Synod meetings, always a welcome, well-heard speaker, no matter where in the state he would be. He was a man of little formal education, but as a delegate to the General Assembly on one occasion, he did not hesitate to speak—with powerful effect —to that large international gathering.

Ike Gabbard was a gallant gentleman, a man whose utter devotion and service to the Lord was inspiring to all who knew him. But if there were but one Ike Gabbard who might command the attention of a single soul or of a great audience, there were countless other folks among our hills who were vital and real, and their words and their expressions were full measures.

Healin'

Manda Sandlin recalled and wrote down for me some of the old mountain remedies in use before "Aunt Nola" came to Morris Fork.

> For worms in children . . . make some tea from the worm seed plant.
> For measles . . . use tea from boiled sassafras roots or use a blend of sulphur and whiskey in cold water.
> For fever . . . make a hot tea from Black Root.
> For colds . . . and babies with hives . . . make some catnip tea or some tea brewed from a weed called high vine.
> To cure babies with "Thrash," let someone, who's never seen the baby's father, blow in the baby's mouth or let an old man who's not a relative put some water in his shoe, tip it up into the toe three

times and then wash the baby's mouth with this
water.

To bring a boil to a head . . . make a poultice from
Slippery Elm bark.

For kidney trouble . . . use tea made from Queen of the
Meadow plant.

For shingles . . . rub blood from a black cat or black
chicken on the areas affected . . . and to cure a dog
with distemper, steal a neighbor's dish cloth and,
after putting some salve on it, tie it around the
animal's neck.

Workin' and Restin'

While there is probably no such thing as a "typical"
day anywhere in the world, many days in the mountains—
over many years—had been very much like one another . . .

About four a.m., with the roosters crowing and a slim
bit of sunlight beginning to creep through the window (if
there were a window), the man of the house would be apt
to say to his wife, "Well, it's daylight—you'd better get
the fire goin'. We'll have to have a bite to eat. After you
milk an' feed the chickens, the kids will have to get off to
school. Guess you'd better be gettin' up."

Obediently, the "old woman" (so-called by her "old
man") would try to begin her day, even though she was
most likely weary from the tasks of the day before. She
would make a fire in the small stove, many times with in-
adequate green wood. The simple breakfast would be
prepared, and she would then call her husband. Next she
would gather the children together and serve and wait on
the family after they were seated. The men folk were
always served first, the girls helping their mother take care
of them.

Hastily eating a bite, after the men were finished, the
"old woman" would then milk and feed the cow and the
chickens. Coming back to the house, she would strain the
milk and store it in a cool place. Then she would wash the
dishes and care for the smaller children.

77

Trying not to think of her tiredness, she would ask, "Do you need me today?", hoping for a "Nope" answer. Instead, it would often be "Yep—that corn patch has to be finished; we got a lot of hoein' to do. You can bring the baby with you."

Up the hill they would all climb to the corn patch. The woman would spread a quilt on the one little level spot likely available, lay the baby down and say to the other two or three children not yet old enough for school, "You mind the little one and watch her good—don't let her roll off the hill!" Mother would then hoe corn until nearly noon, taking off perhaps two or three little "spurts o' time" to nurse the baby. When the father would say, "Guess we'd better quit 'n eat," she would gather up the baby and wearily descend the hill. Another fire would have to be made in the little stove for preparing the noon meal. The father would soon find a chair and a cool place in the shade, where he would rest after his hard morning's work.

Then, after the midday meal, back to the corn field for everyone. The mother would work until around five p.m., or whenever the "old man" would say, "Guess it's time to quit—I shore am tired! We got to do our chores. After you do the milkin and get supper, 'twill be pretty nigh dark." So, down the hill one more time and off to the barn for milking and feeding, then one more meal to cook and the children to care for.

This was pretty much the routine of the summer, with work in the garden thrown in. In the fall, the gathering of the crops as well as canning, drying and "pickling" of vegetables . . . all these were mostly the "old woman's" job. How the housework was done, and sewing, washing and ironing, was sometimes a womanly mystery.

The "old man?" Well, he did care for his mules or horses. And there was always much "tinkering" to be done, with the wagon, the home-made sled, the fences. He was indeed head of the house. He had to oversee all that was going on. In the early years, there was much logging that meant taking rafts down the river where the logs would be sold in markets such as Frankfort. These rafts were made of logs nailed together. The men would stand on them and propel them with poles for the many long miles.

The "old man's" taking care of the family often included "takin kere" of his neighbors. One father told me that he was so bothered by a neighbor he decided to "settle him" once and for all. Before either realized it, a real mountain feud had developed. Each was "shore goin to get" the other. Deeper and deeper the feelings went, until this father decided he had to have the right sort of a gun to do the job. What he wanted he couldn't find close by. So, one morning he said to his wife, "I got business to do, I'm going away for a few days. You take care o' things 'til I git back." And he started his long walk of sixty miles from Crocketsville to Winchester, to find just the type of gun he needed.

The complete trip of a fortnight accomplished, he loaded his specially purchased weapon and sought out his neighbor. He found him working in his field. "Now I've got him!" he thought. He cocked the new gun, aimed and pulled the trigger—but it didn't fire! Three times he tried, but with no luck. Finally, throwing the gun on the ground, he lifted his eyes heavenward and said: "Alright, God—if you don't want me to shoot him, I won't!"

The two men came across the corn field towards each other, one waving his handkerchief and shouting wildly. "Come on—I ain't going to shoot!" They shook hands, and the feud was ended.

79

"STARTING TO COMMENCE
TO BEGIN"

1927-1939

In our early months at Morris Fork, it was not unusual for us to find ourselves with no cash whatsoever. There was certainly no "foundation" behind us, or any "government aid." We even did without outside church or other help. Because Sam was not a seminary graduate, our church board would not recognize or support him. At the time of our marriage, my commission from our National Board of Missions was discontinued—as was my $50.00 monthly salary. Even Sam's pittance from Buckhorn ended because of budget shortcomings there. And, from that day in June, until November, there was no "salary"—no cash income from anywhere—no church, no government, no one behind us. Did I say no one behind us? *"Consider the lilies of the field, how they grow, they toil not, neither do they spin, and yet I say unto you that even Solomon, in all his glory, was not arrayed like one of these. Wherefore, if God so clothe the grass of the field, which today and tomorrow is cast into the oven, shall he not much more clothe you, O ye of little faith?"*

Financial blessings came our way from time to time. One of these, a rather large bill, arrived in a blank envelope from Louisville. To this day, I do not know who sent it.

How generous our own Morris Fork folks quickly became with their gifts of vegetables, eggs, chickens, and fresh meat, butchered from their own hogs. Their gifts of labor and materials made possible all the buildings we began to construct.

All these gifts were, they said, "in pay" for our coming and for all we were doing. Our faith was strengthened day by day, as our needs were met and rich promises were fulfilled.

In our first November, we received an interesting message from a Presbyterian church in Newark, New Jersey. "We had a missionary in Kentucky," it said, "but that work is closed. We wonder if you would like to be our missionaries?" Then the letter added . . . "Could we come down to see you?" We responded with an enthusiastic, "Yes!"

And so the minister and a few other representatives of the Forest Hills Presbyterian Church journeyed to meet us . . . and Morris Fork. The trip, most especially the horseback portion of it, was an adventure for them. They were appalled at the conditions and needs they saw, but were impressed by our first efforts to deal with them. "We want to support you," they said. "We will provide you with $125.00 each month, if that will help." Sam and I looked at each other, the same thought in our hearts. "Lo, I am with you always . . . " Help indeed!

So began our nearly forty years of friendship with the folks at Forest Hills, a friendship that would be dramatically consummated soon when the time came to build our church. They often supplemented the regular support with special purchases of medical supplies, or something else we especially needed. But just as importantly, members of the church came to visit us—to lend heart and hands to our work. We became busy and happy partners in the deepest sense. Whenever possible, Sam and I would make a journey of our own back to New Jersey to help renew the bonds of fellowship between our two churches. These were always joyous occasions.

Sam had, of course, done some teaching roundabout Morris Fork. But when he contacted the Breathitt County Superintendent of Schools to ask about having a regular school program, he was told, "It's okay, but we can't pay anything, and we can't give you any supplies. You are not a certified teacher."

Nevertheless, with a Calfey's Rural Arithmetic, a Sears Roebuck catalogue, and a New Testament, the school began. It was absolutely amazing what geography, reading, and math one could get from that Sears catalogue!

Soon the parents asked if they could come, too! Illiteracy was so very high, for there had been no schools anywhere around.

Sam had stuffed the cracks and chinks in the tired little building that was used, but with few supplies it seemed almost impossible to think about adding more "pupils." But the request was not dropped. In our Community League, where all questions of state were settled, the project was discussed, "We ain't never had no chance to go to school—but we want to know how to read and write."

The "almost impossible" was just that—the Morris Fork Moonlight School was organized! There was barely time for Sam to get home after the children left the schoolroom, to do his chores, have a bite to eat, and get back for the oldsters. They just couldn't be too late or too long away from their little homes.

Darkness came early in the hills, and, in spite of all our planning and scheming, 'twas the "edge of night" before many could get to the little schoolhouse. So what did we do? Well, the folks solved part of the problem by making and carrying torches! These were real torches of wood which they gathered from the hills. They would be lighted, and burned as they walked through the hills to and from the schoolhouse. A few had lanterns. Inside the little building, we used kerosene lamps, as many as we could "scrape up."

What nights these were! Happy, joyous laughter and competition, as one after another took on readin', writin', and 'rithmetic. There were spelling bees, reading contests, and some fifteen to twenty mothers and fathers had their first experience of "get-to-getherness."

When the editors of *Our Appalachia* compiled their fine oral history, they included a conversation with Sam. In one part of it, he spoke about his first "moonlight school" days:

> . . . These fathers and mothers in the night school amazed me by their ability to learn, and I realized the potential of the mountain people. There was one grandmother who was seventy, named Kate Helton.

Kate came every night, her eyesight was poor, but she came up that creek. Kate would try awfully hard and it was a thrill to her when she learned to add one column of figures on the blackboard, and then two columns of figures, and then we got into subtraction. I'll never forget the night when we started long division with these adults. Poor Kate pushed her glasses in every conceivable position and she took the piece of chalk and she chewed on it and she looked at the problem and said, "Sam, I've gone as far as I can go. I can't do this." I said, "Kate, you've done all the others, you can do it," and she mastered it.

At the end of the school I had the thrill of being at her home. She said to her husband, who was the postmaster, "John, I want you to go down the creek and measure that log. I want you to tell me how long it is and how big it is through the butt." He measured it. Then she said, "Now, get me a paper poke." John brought her a paper poke. Kate fished in her pocket where she carried her revolver, and her twist of tobacco, and she pulled out a little piece of pencil and she chewed on it, she told him exactly how many board feet there'd be on that log. [Then] John measured the wagon bed and she told him how many tons of coal it would hold. John was just amazed: "Where did you learn that?" She said, "I learned that at the night school. You laughed at me for going."

The "moonlight school" was a wonderful opening wedge. It helped us to make friends with children and parents, to reach into homes. So many good things really began with it.

Almost immediately we also began a sanitary privy project, necessary because of the very unsanitary conditions around the homes. There were no privies of any description, no signs of a "shack out back." Realizing that such conditions were responsible for much of the sickness and infection prevalent, we knew they could not be ignored. Someone suggested a contest. Would "Up-Creekers" or "Down-Creekers" have the most toilets first?

Each Sunday, before our worship service, posters that had been made were held up and read, and announcements about sanitary improvements were made. Strict attention was paid to the directions we had obtained from the State Board of Health for privy construction. Holes had to be just so deep and lined with concrete and rock. Securing the concrete was a real problem. "Working it" right was another. The aim was to see which families could have their "little houses" completely finished first. How everyone worked in the friendly competition. And how proud we were when the final results came. Practically all our families completed their project in keeping with state requirements.

What had God wrought!

From Miss McCord and Wooton, we had learned the worth of having a community house that we could make the focal point of our assorted activities. As soon as it was possible to gather men and materials to construct one, we did just that. On its completion, we made the second floor our home.

Before even the hint of any sort of a washer came to us, we heated water in a big kettle right on the creek bank. We scrubbed our clothes on a board, boiled 'em with good homemade soap, and hung 'em on an outside line—"the prettiest wash you ever did see." Ironing was done with heavy flatirons, heated on a coal-burning stove, if we were lucky enough to have such a luxury. But many times, the sooty, coal-burning fireplace was used. Then, of course, "smudgy ironing" resulted.

We had, early on, a dug well just outside the downstairs porch that afforded a good supply of water for many of our needs. But because Sam and I lived on the second floor of the community house, all our water had to be carried, not merely in and out—but up and down!

Eventually, we decided to afford water in the kitchen with a pump. Such proceedings as took place to bring this about! Just finding the necessary pipe, sink fixtures, and the pump itself was quite a challenge. "We'll help put it in," our men said, "but 'tain't nary use to try this—hit just won't work."

With all these doubting Thomases, and their skeptical eyes watching every move, the pump was finally installed. When it seemed to be ready, Sam said to "Uncle Sol" Riley, "Here's a glass, you get the first drink."

Sam began pumping vigorously. When the first water gushed out, "Uncle Sol" dropped the glass! A look of complete amazement fairly bugged his eyes.

"Well, by doggies!" everyone exclaimed.

As the late autumn arrived, Sam and I planned and worked to bring all we could of Christmas to Morris Fork. We simply could not realize that this was to be the very first Christmas for these folks. They did not know the Christmas story—the old, old Christmas carols—all the beauty and wonder and meaning of our Saviour's birth. Christmas had only been a time of more bootleggings, more shootings, more terror up and down the creeks. Surely this could never be again! And so with more hard work, prayer, explaining "what this is all about," we plunged into plans for the first Morris Fork Christmas.

As the season drew near, we stretched our meager finances, which seemed as nothing toward a holiday sharing with some 500 folks—especially folks who would be experiencing Christmas for the first time. Word of our needs had not yet reached many outside churches, and we were not receiving much help. Some boxes of gifts had come, especially used clothing. This clothing was a motley lot—all kinds and all sizes, with much variety in quality. All night long Sam and I worked—sorting, tagging, wrapping—just the two of us, trying to find and make a Christmas package for everyone. This first Christmas we had no church, but a decorated tree was ready on the lawn and the unpredictable Kentucky weather was unusually warm. The Christmas party was set up outdoors, but first more than 100 people squeezed into our living room for a very special service.

We had known only too well that our folks had no

money either for giving, or buying gifts, but we did want them to begin to know the joy of remembering Christ's birthday with sharing—not just receiving. We were all short of worldly goods, but so were many others outside our little settlement. How could we do this? Suddenly we remembered the manger. Why couldn't we make a manger offering? We knew our families all grew corn; so we asked that each bring an ear of corn wrapped in white paper, with the total amount of corn they were willing to give—a bushel, half bushel, even just numbers of ears—written on the paper. For the value of the pledges of corn, we would take cash from the monetary support we received and send it to the missions. The corn pledges would sometimes be redeemed in nice sweet corn for use on community occasions. How beautifully folks responded as we joyfully sang, "O Come All Ye Faithful," while the white gifts were placed in the manger as offerings to the Christ Child . . . and the meaning of Christmas grew.

We couldn't know that as we made this first Christmas a part of a letter to our loved ones, friends and supporters far away, we were beginning another tradition. The letter of each year that followed, like this first letter, recalled the Christmas season and the year that had passed. Strung together, these letters—down through the one from our last winter at Morris Fork in 1968—are something of a chronicle of those many wonderful years. Parts of some of them are among the pages to come. But a small glimpse—back to that first Christmas of 1927—recalls for me just how special and exciting it was . . .

"Silent Night, Holy Night, All is Calm, All is Bright." It was the closing scene of the sacred pageant "God's Gift of Love." The cast, our mountain young people and some of the parents, had walked three miles over the mountain to give the pageant, at their request, to the folks of the neighboring community where there was less doing for Christmas. The hastily improvised "stage," the porch of the little schoolhouse, answered our purpose nicely. The audience, some two

86

hundred and fifty of our mountain folks, were grouped in the yard. How thankful we were for mild weather, for we could not have seated such a crowd in the small school building.

The manger scene was the closing scene. For more than an hour the people had stood (there was no way to seat such a crowd) and listened to the wonderful Christmas story. Ever wonderful, but how much more so to those who were hearing it, in such a way, for the first time. The hidden choir of young people had learned the beautiful Christmas carols for the first time also, but the music of their voices almost belied the fact. A pause, and as "O Come All Ye Faithful" was heard, the wise men and shepherds, with their oriental costumes and "crooks," entered the scene and kneeled around the manger. Another pause, then as the whole mountainside seemed to echo the glad message, "Joy to the World," the entire cast gathered around the manger. A joyous thrill went through the audience and the rapt attention that had reached a degree of intensity gave way with a sign of peace and contentment; we knew that our people had understood and loved this way of telling the Christmas story. Back into the Old Testament we had gone, and one prophecy after another was fulfilled until we were brought right up to the manger scene itself. "Why, I could have stood and listened to that over and over again," one man said.

"Joy to the World." The Christ Child had come to Morris Fork.

With our growing program of activities, the community house, which was our home and only gathering place, quickly became far too small. It was even our house of worship on Sunday—there was nowhere else to go. Sunday school classes were conducted in the bedrooms, living room, kitchen, on the steps, even in the yard. We decided we must have a real sure-enough church; it would be our largest undertaking.

Talking with our folks about it, they asked, "What is a church for? Why do we have to have one?"

Uncle Sam tried to explain. "A church is a building that especially belongs to God. Here we will come to worship Him, to study the Bible, to learn more about Him. We will have a Sunday School where boys and girls can learn about Him, and a church group especially for our young people. We can use the church in many ways to honor and serve God; it will be a light in this community showing that we are Christians."

"Alrighty, we'll help all we can to build one," they responded. "When can we start?"

There were many meetings, discussions and plans—and pledges of labor and materials.

Then came the question of money. We had to have some cash, beyond these gifts offered by our people. But cash we had not. So we decided to go to our friends at the Forest Hills Presbyterian Church in Newark to talk of our hopes.

"Charlie Turner has given the gift of enough land," we said, "and our people have offered labor and materials. But we do need some ready cash. Could you perhaps help us?" Our pleas were made in a meeting with the Forest Hills Church session.

Could they—would they—help? What a blessed memory is the beautiful, ready and loving response that came. "We are so happy to have this privilege to help build a church where there never has been one! Will five thousand dollars do for a starter?"

Our exciting task began! It was entirely a local project. Sam drew all the plans and explained them to our men. Without the help of any trained specialists in architecture or construction, it was marvelous how the building progressed. Aside from a small "handmade" mill that could saw logs, there was no machinery of any description. Lumber and stones came directly from the hills; the huge trees cut by our men, the rocks and stones dug out by hand. All were hauled from the hills by our faithful mules and horses. The roof and sides of the building were all covered with hand-cut shingles.

The gift acres of land had to be put in shape also by hand and mule power. Large, rough rocks brought from the creeks and hills were cut and hand-chiseled by "Rock George" Riley. Once a moonshiner and considered illiterate, Rock George completed the most fantastic, unbelievable job of fashioning these rocks into foundation stones, fireplaces, chimneys—whatever stonework was needed. "I'm proud to do it," he would say, his merry eyes twinkling. "Didn't know I could do ary a thing like this!" And as he kept at it, over the months of building, we marvelled again: "What hath God wrought?"

Our initial construction included the sanctuary and the Sunday School room; later a primary room and three other classrooms were added. Two hundred chairs were made by hand for our Sunday School room! Two lovely pulpits, our choir benches, our tables—were also handmade. We did purchase pews and some flooring. But aside from this, all materials came from our hills. Piece by piece, laboriously but lovingly, how the building did progress, and "The Little Brown Church" become visible.

During the building of the church, a bunch of men from the other side of the creek came riding up our way. Hearing the hammering and pounding, one of them exclaimed, "They must be making a *real* still at Morris Fork this time!" Coming closer and into the grounds, they couldn't believe their eyes. "What? . . . a church? . . . not a still? Whatever has happened to these folks?"

Lighting the church without electricity posed a special problem.

"Can you get several old wagon wheels?" asked Sam.

"What in the world do you want with them?" the men asked.

"Well," he replied, "we have to have some lights . . . "

"I'll be hanged," one replied, scratching his head, "But if you needs 'em, we'll get 'em."

After quite a search, eight old lumber wagon wheels appeared. Very carefully they were taken apart, scrubbed, put back together, creosoted and fitted with candles. Then they were hung in the sanctuary. Others were prepared the same way for the Sunday School room.

Since the land given by Charlie Turner for the church was almost barren woodland, there was a need for considerable landscaping, and beautifying with greenery of one sort or another. "We must make the outside as lovely as the inside," Sam said.

All that we needed for this was everywhere roundabout us . . . rhododendron, holly, pine trees, azaleas . . . all so beautiful and all "free for nuthin." Once again, man and beast took to the hills and helped to make our little plot "blossom like a rose."

As the church itself grew to look more and more like a church . . . with its tall natural pillars in the sanctuary and its lovely handhewn shingles outside . . . we couldn't help but marvel at the achievement. All this, designed by an "architect" who had never seen a book on architecture and built by men who trusted his ideas and plans. "We're not sure what it's going to look like, but if you say so, we'll do it."

At last—there was the beautiful, rustic church, all of native timbers and stones from our hills, built with the loving labor of all Morris Forkers. What an answer to prayer! The tall pillars and overhead beams in the sanctuary, the homemade tables, pulpit furniture, chairs and choir benches—all told of His great love and a wonderful opportunity we'd had of "doing it together."

What a thrilling time it was when our "little brown church in the wildwood" was ready for dedication.

My mother and father journeyed all the way from Illinois for the dedication service, and my father himself gave the dedicatory sermon.

The dedication exercises began with some two hundred of us gathering at the old "shambly" schoolhouse by the creek, where we had most recently been holding our services. The primary level children led the procession, carrying their little handmade chairs with them. The choir followed—then everybody . . . all singing joyously "Lead On O King Eternal."

What a triumphant and joyful experience, as we marched from one sacred spot to another . . . sacred because even in the old schoolhouse, many had found their Savior. 'Twas here we had "started to commence to begin."

Our Lord had blest without measure. Tears of joy and happiness overflowed as we marched from the old to the new. Memories—and expectations—filled our hearts to overflowing.

This church—our church—the very first, not only for Morris Fork but for miles around, dedicated to His glory and our commitment to Christian living and service.

After our moving dedicatory service, there was of course a big and festive community dinner, with folks bringing all their "fixins." Then much hymn singing and testimonies and pledges for rededicated Christian life.

The little brown church is still "a lighthouse that cannot be hid," where many folks gather each week to renew their commitment to a life more abundant.

Soon after arriving at Morris Fork as a bride, I realized there was no such thing as "social standing." Everybody was like everybody else. All of us were poor, but we didn't know it! Being poor put us on the same level; we were all simply folks. No one had electricity, no one had running water, no one had a bathroom, and no one had a refrigerator. And there were no maids to help with the children or the housework! There were no Joneses to keep up with or to envy each day. We counted the blessings we had—and we shared them.

In a community where the money flow was practically nil, now did folks "make it?" There were no banks anywhere around for bank accounts, even if there had been dollars for them. When there was a bit of extra cash, it was hidden under a mattress, in a jar, "put away good," or simply carried in apron or overall pockets.

We all lived by bartering, and it worked well. We

The Little Brown Church

*The Morris Fork Church as originally constructed by our men.
An addition to meet growth of Sunday School was made later.*

*Men of the church—many of them its builders. "Rock George"
Riley is fifth from right.*

Note the hand cut timbers and wagon wheel light—in this interior view of the church.

"SAMINOLA"

When a man bearing the name of Samuel VanderMeer appeared in the mountains, he himself was not only an utter stranger; his name itself was strange to the likes of the Morrises, Turners, Deatons and Rileys of Morris Fork.

"We just can't say your name," they complained.

"Why, that's all right," he said. "Just call me 'Uncle Sam.' Think you can remember that?" And "Uncle Sam" it was. After our marriage, "Aunt Nola" was simply inevitable.

After a few years of very active involvement, Sam became the state Christian Endeavor president. While he was on the platform once to receive a presentation, he asked me to join him. In our introduction, someone said,

"Since Sam and Nola are working together, it seems like a combination name might be good and helpful. Why don't we just call this fine team, 'Saminola'?"

And so, separately and jointly, we were named . . . for all the mountain years that followed.

found that money was not a necessary commodity. There were times when bartering seemed to get "rather hot," especially with sharp dealings involving horses or mules, or when there were cow "trade-ins," but in general it made for friendly contacts among neighbors.

The corn which was raised on every farm was food for both animals and folks, but it was also central to bartering. Each Saturday, a grist of whole corn was taken to the nearest mill, sometimes many miles away. This was carried by horse or mule back. The mill owner would take out a portioned amount of the whole corn or ground meal as "pay." This was done weekly all through the mountains and was a way of obtaining meal for home use and . . . for currency!

There was, of course, no machinery of any kind. If a person didn't own a "working mule," he waited until a neighbor could help plow and work the garden with *his*. Through the late summer and fall, great quantities of vegetables were canned and dried. Potatoes, cabbages and turnips were "hoed up" in deep holes in the garden, where the frost couldn't get 'em—and left safe for winter use. Luscious sweet potatoes were a big part of these "hoed away goodies." They were white and fluffy "sweets," not the soggy sort generally found in supermarkets today.

Nor did we want for beauty.

A couple of years or so after all the landscaping with trees, shrubs and flowers had been completed in the church and Community House yard, Aunt Sally Riley seemed to be enjoying a bit of wandering about in it. The rhododendron was in its full glory, dressed in beautiful pink and white blooms.

"Oh, Uncle Sam!" Sally exclaimed. "Where did you get such beautiful flowers? They musta cost a heap o'money. I never did see anything so purty."

"Why, Aunt Sally, shame on you!" Sam replied. "You've lived with these all your life. They came from the mountainside there, across the creek. Just look around and see all the beauty God has given us in our hills."

As work progressed during the early years, our program enlarged, and we soon began receiving many gifts of clothing for our folks. These came as other churches and groups began to learn of "Morris Fork." This clothing was a wonderful boon. Much of the time, folks would come to us and tell us of their special needs. We would give them what we could from this supply. At other times, those who could pay for things with eggs, meat, potatoes did so. We did not "pauperize." We knew our folks wanted the dignity of exchanging what they had for what we had. And we were thankful to have their offerings so that these could be shared.

When medical help was given, or medical supplies provided, we felt, too, there would be more self-respect retained if a minimum "price" were asked. There were many, many friendly visits made in times of sickness, when no "pay" was expected, and many baby deliveries made with no charge. But we did come to a set $5.00 fee for a delivery. This included not only the delivery but a baby layette and care for the mother and babe for ten days. I'd return to take care of the baby, bathe the mother, leave her in a fresh nightie and clean bed and oftentimes do a big "washin.'"

One day, when I was making my last visit to see a mother, I found her in bed waiting for me. After her bath and my departure, a neighbor said, "Did you know Sally was at the barn milkin' when you came? She saw you comin' and ran to the house and got in bed. She just wanted one more nice bath."

Most of our medical supplies in later years came from the Eli Lilly Co. in Indianapolis, through our good friends in the suburban Southport Church who obtained them at wholesale prices. As the supplies were used at Morris Fork, we would frequently receive eggs or the like in payment. Whenever we did "barter" with eggs, chickens or vegetables, we always tried to make it an even exchange.

One Sunday, after a service, a very small girl came to Uncle Sam and gave him a penny. "What's this for, Honey?" he asked. "That's your pay," she replied.

At one point, we became acutely aware of our need for

a horse. We didn't want to be beggars, but there just wasn't money for such an acquisition. Back in New Jersey, nephew Lambert learned of our need. As he'd see folks in the family, he would ask, "You know Sam VanderMeer?"

"Yes," would of course be the answer.

"Well, that will cost you $10." Sam's famous namesake nephew, Johnny (Samuel) VanderMeer, recalls being among those captured for donations.

Soon the money came for our horse! As in the time of Elisha, it seemed, over and over, that the oil and meal "wasted not." Our Lord did provide!

A friend who had a farm outside Lexington brought us a dozen fresh eggs, which she left casually on the kitchen table. Underneath one of the eggs was a $50 bill! "Hannah," I said, "I sure would like to know what kind of chickens you have, that lay those kinds of eggs!"

The gifts of clothing and our increasing volume of mail required acknowledgement. Without it, our friends would wonder why we didn't appreciate their interest and help. I'd never had a single lesson in typing, but many times I found myself at the typewriter past midnight, doing my best—hunting, pecking . . . and thanking.

As for building and maintenance . . . well, Lambert loves to recall the time "Uncle Sam just managed to take me for a stroll out to the old shed at the rear of the church. And right there, wouldn't you know, he found five 5-gallon cans of brown paint that had started to rust up. We opened one of them and found the paint fine, and just waiting to be used. I was awarded the contract of painting the church!"

Of course, there were no cleaning gadgets. We simply swept, dusted, mopped and scrubbed. Usually the rough floors were scrubbed with homemade soap and water, a la one's hands and knees! Heating water on a stove for everything was a big item. And where there were children, as there generally were, it seemed huge.

Weekly "janitoring" of the church came to be a regular part of our community housekeeping. The folks helped with this, each family taking turns, sweeping, dusting, mopping. Most of our little "stores" kept an adequate supply of kerosene, but broken chimneys for our lamps were not always easy to replace. Keeping the lamps of both the church and community house in working order—with clean chimneys—was no small task. And the outside toilets had to be kept in "first class order." Many times, being away a night or two for a "baby case" meant that the housekeeping posed a real problem. Secretly, on my return, I wished at some times for electricity and the other conveniences of the world outside.

Because Sam was not a Seminary graduate, the Presbyterian Board of National Missions had not recognized us enough to help in any financial way, but they were in correspondence with us, and every once in a while would send a "drop in" representative to call on me. "Am on my way elsewhere, but came near Morris Fork and thought I'd drop in and see you." With our modest income stretched as it was, we were perplexed and somewhat amused whenever this particular demand was made upon it.

An occasion of this sort occurred one summer, by surprise, and "smack dab" in the middle of our canning and drying season. We had been notified to expect our New York Board visitors on Thursday. This gave us the first days of the week, so we thought, to take care of a great tub of green beans and some housecleaning.

All of a sudden—right in the midst of some Monday bean stringin'—our mailman arrived on horseback with a telegram: "HAVE DECIDED TO COME EARLIER. WILL BE AT MORRIS FORK MONDAY NIGHT." We were flabbergasted! What to do? What to prepare?

In a quandary, and rather breathlessly, I hailed one of our mothers, who was passing by . . . "Have just had word we're getting visitors for supper. Don't have anything to give them. Could you maybe dress me a couple of fryers and bring them over right away?"

"Why, sure enough," she answered.

After more breathlessness—and hustlin' and bustlin', the fried chicken dinner was ready.

98

But on seeing the results of our heroic efforts, one of our prominent guests exclaimed, "You know, I never eat chicken."

"Well," I responded, "I'm sorry, but there just is no place around here to get anything else . . . Would you like me to make you a peanut butter sandwich?"

When Lambert VanderMeer was about seventeen, he decided to strike out from New Jersey by train—by horse—and by foot, for a surprise visit with us at Morris Fork.

"I don't remember just where the train left me off, but after walking a considerable distance, I found that I was about six miles from Morris Fork. I had stopped to ask a couple of fellows for some directions. Well, right away they thought I was a Revenue man. They searched me, and to have me prove that I wasn't, they had me drink some of their 'corn.' When I did, I broke out in a cold sweat and grew very weak in the knees. I guess they were satisfied that I was unacquainted with their world."

Folks raised their corn, and it was theirs to do with as they pleased! Whose business was it if it were made into moonshine? Grandfathers before them had made it, and their grandfathers too. And it brought in at least some little income. But we were *agin* it, as well our folks came to know. And we were "agin" it because of a tragic kind of scene we described in our letter about Christmas Day of 1927 . . .

On Christmas Day, after our exercises, a crowd of men, not of our own community, started up the creek where all knew that "moonshine" could be had. About midnight we were awakened with the report that a man, one of that very group, had been killed in a drunken brawl. How our hearts ached! The tragedy had happened at a near neighbor's home, where the man who was shot, with his brother, had come for protection from another man who was crazy with drink. All three had been drinking, and a quarrel had started. The man and his brother had taken the other man's

99

high powered gun and fled. In the meantime, the other man rushed into a neighbor's house, took a pistol by force, ran back to hunt his companions and fired the fatal shots. The victim lived about eight hours, suffering intensely. We talked to him about his need of the Saviour and read and prayed with him. His wife and four small children are left alone with absolutely nothing to meet their needs, and another little one will soon be added to the group.

The murderer was taken to our county jail, to await trial. His wife had fled from the house during the fight and spent the night in a shock of fodder. The next morning, she was found, so frightened and cold that she could scarcely move. The temperature was down to about five above zero.

The morning after Christmas, a raid was made, with the result that the stills were smashed and one of our leading moonshiners is now a fugitive from justice.

On the same day of our tragedy, word came from our county seat that a frenzied mob took from the jail a prisoner, who a few days previous had shot down a man in cold blood. The fifteen year old son of the dead man was in the masked mob. The prisoner's body was riddled with bullets, and he was then thrown over a cliff into a creek. Here he was found. He regained consciousness and told the names of the men in the mob. Now he has gone into eternity. "Bloody Breathitt." For years it has carried this well deserved title, but let us not forget that in the World War Breathitt's men volunteered 100%. Why not aim for 100% for Christ? "Overcome evil with good." The Bible is true, and we have proved that this is the surest way. So while we are rejoicing in our wonderful Christmas time, and send our friends our heartiest appreciation, we just want you to realize with us the crying need of our hills. We appreciate more than we can tell you your living interest and help and covet your continued prayers. *Inasmuch as ye have done it unto one of the least of these, ye have done it unto Me.*

Bill Morris was an older man, and Sam was immediately drawn to him. He was so kindly, and he could talk of so many different things. He was interested in his family and sympathetic with the work of the church. He had even helped in its building. But Bill was a moonshiner and everyone knew it. "I can't quit," he said. "My grandpappy did hit; hit's just in me." "I like you, and I'll keep on praying," Sam told him. Bill just smiled.

But one night, Bill's moonshining stopped abruptly.

Once in a while, the "revenooers" came up and down the creeks, and this time they found Bill, at his still.

"You have to get me out of this!" Bill entreated Sam. "I just can't leave my family and go to jail." But he was convicted and given a five-year sentence in the Federal prison. Over and over his wife would come to the house. "Uncle Sam, won't you please help me get Bill out of jail? I need him; he must come back to his family." "I'm so sorry," Sam would reply. "I tried to get him to stop before they caught him. He wouldn't, and now he must pay for his wrong. I can't help you get him out, but I will pray the Lord will speak to him and he'll come home a changed man." "That would be good," she replied, "but there ain't ary a chance o' that. Bill will always moonshine. I need him so bad!"

About three years later, a wonderful letter came from Bill. "Sam, I'm 'payrolled'! I'm comin home, and I'm a different man. I found Christ in a Salvation Army meeting the other night. I'm a Christian—I'm comin home to help you and my family. And I'll never touch moonshine again!"

What a blessing Bill was when he returned! Joybells were certainly ringing everywhere. "Sam, Sam, I've been such a wicked man. How can I ever make up for all this? I want to go to Sunday School with you and tell all the young men what a fool I've been. They must not do what I've done. I want to help win them for Christ. I've hurt too many." Soon, he was an elder in the little church. The Sunday he was baptized, a great crowd gathered. Sam generally "sprinkled" our adults as well as our babies and children; but Bill wanted immersion! We sang joyfully and lustily, as he went into the creek. A little bunch of folks under the trees were heard to say, "He doesn't mean it! He'll never stick to it. Wait and see, he'll be right back at that still."

But Bill never did go back to his still. Sam took him to a Synod meeting of our church in Harlan. As they were going down the aisle, he stopped. He said in a hoarse voice, "Sam, look there! That's a police officer; he said he was going to get me dead or alive!" Sam wondered just what sort of a Synod meeting this would turn out to be. But he persuaded Bill to sit down. After the service, this man did spy Bill. Coming up to him, he said, "What are you doing here?" "I'm representing my church," Bill replied; "what are *you* doing here?" With a smile he said, "Same thing!" They shook hands and walked out arm in arm.

Bill was indeed faithful to his promise. Never did he seem so happy as when he was going with Sam to our various Sunday school groups, talking especially to the boys and young men about the "better life." "Don't get with the wrong company," he warned. "Don't ever get mixed up with the whiskey business. What trouble 'twould have saved me if I hadn't. And what dishonor to my Lord. Boys, listen to me: I know what I'm telling you is the truth. My brother Jeff, I've got to stop him; he cannot go on with his hellish business."

But Jeff would hear none of such talk. He did not openly fight us, he was friendly when we talked to him, but he had nothing to do with any church activities—never attended a service.

"Aunt Mary," Jeff's wife, did become interested. She lived some three miles from the church, up one of the roughest creeks and hollows we had. Before long, bless her heart, she became one of our regular Sunday school and church attendants. Every Sunday she would come, many times through drenching rain or summer heat or snow storms, walking those rough miles to the church and then home again. Always in spring, summer and fall, she would carry a bunch of flowers or a "pretty bush" gathered as she walked. If there were no flowers, there

102

would be grasses or weeds she admired. "I just think they look pretty," she would say.

One time a group of people came to Sam saying, "You know Mary Morris is helping Jeff moonshine? Everyone knows she does just about as much of it as he! She shouldn't be allowed in the church as long as she keeps this up. We think you'd better tell her we know she's a hypocrite, and we don't want her." Sam was so hurt . . . but it didn't take him long to give them illustrations from the Bible of God's love for all people, that all are sinners and come short of the glory of God. "This is what His church is for: to save sinners like you and me . . . and Mary. We must keep on praying for her and loving her. And Jeff, too. Don't ever tell her she can't come to our little church." And sure enough, it was not too many months until Mary united with the church. "I want to quit my bad ways; I want Christ to forgive and help me; I want to follow Him."

Still, Jeff kept at his moonshining, till about three years later when he himself followed Mary into the church. "I too want to follow Christ," he said. "I want Him to forgive my sin of moonshining. I ain't never goin' to do it no more."

"Uncle Jeff," Sam asked, "What made you finally quit?" "Why," he answered, "I heered you folks here at the church was prayin' for me. I couldn't fight all them prayers."

Only a few years after our tragedy-scarred Christmas of 1927, we would write of change . . . joyful change.

"Ring out the Old, ring in the New." For the first time in history, a church bell on Morris Fork blended its joyful notes with thousands of others all through the country, welcoming the New Year!

New Year's Eve had been spent in the Community Room in a quiet peaceful way. About fifty boys and girls, young folks and parents had gathered for the evening. They were told not to come too early, for we were having open house until midnight, but at five the first installment had arrived! We looked forward to the hours rather wearily.

The first part of the evening was spent with quiet table games—the folks are just beginning to understand and enjoy these, and this evening they enjoyed them to the full. Small tables had been placed in the room and on each table was a tall red candle. They played so happily and quietly that we gasped when we realized that it was ten o'clock! The tables were then pushed back and the chairs grouped around the piano near the log fire. Hot coffee, milk, sandwiches and candy were served and at ten forty-five we began our service. One after another told of leaving a life of sin and living a life with Christ the past year—and the radiant glowing faces strengthened the testimony that the past year with Christ had been one of joy and blessing and the old days were gone forever! Many took in the prayer service, some praying publicly for the first time. It was a time of reconsecration, and as we entered the New Year on our knees, we felt it would hold many wonderful things for our Community. Then the church bell pealed forth and with thanksgiving in our hearts we welcomed 1931.

At the New Year's Day dinner, there was some straightforward talk regarding the needs of our community and the obligations we as Christians should assume toward meeting these needs. The result was that each one present, with hand uplifted in the presence of God, pledged himself to loyalty to the work of the Church, his Community and his Country. And for those who have relatives still in the "moonshine business," this pledge meant reporting and not shielding the offenders . . .

Frank Hersman was an old family friend from Illinois. In a warm and interesting piece he wrote about Morris Fork and shared with us in 1952, he recounted one experience that stood out especially for him—an experience that seems like a benediction to the story of "The Last Moonshiner" . . .

On World Communion Sunday we were in the

beautiful, rustic Morris Fork Church. After the worship period the Pastor came down from the pulpit and stood by the Lord's Table. I cannot remember his exact words but I shall never forget the sacredness of that hour.

He said something like this:

"This morning I come to the Lord's table remembering. I come remembering the first Lord's Supper with His twelve disciples. I come remembering my first communion when I joined the Church and the one when I was ordained a Presbyterian Minister. I come remembering Jeff Morris, our last moonshiner, who is one of our Elders who will help serve communion today.

"I could have gone out into the garden this morning for fresh flowers to intertwine with those sourwood branches on the wall above the choir. But instead I used wilted flowers kept over from the Fair of last Friday, because this morning I come to the Lord's Table remembering the broken lives of our community that have been made whole by our Saviour."

A "proper wedding," one with a real service and with all the "trimmings," had never taken place at Morris Fork.

Soon after the completion of our church, a young girl announced she was going to get married. This seemed like our opportunity! Talking to her and her parents—the boy was "on a job" in Ohio, and we couldn't see him—we tried to explain and to picture for them the beauty of a simple wedding in the church. Alpha was certainly interested. She said she'd love being married in the church.

So wedding plans were made. We obtained a piece of silk, and the mothers got together to make the very first wedding gown! The wedding was to take place Saturday afternoon. On Friday, the last rehearsal, with all its important directions, began. The groom had not as yet appeared from his job in Ohio, but Alpha marched down the aisle in her wedding gown to the very first strains of the wedding march ever heard in that whole vicinity. She was radiant, and final instructions were given.

Saturday morning a visitor came to the community house. Amidst other conversation, the wedding was mentioned. "You'll be coming?" I asked. "They are going to be married in the church today."

"Why, didn't you know, Alpha was married last night?"

"Oh, no," I replied. "That's a mistake. They are coming to the church this afternoon; we have it all planned."

But the visitor insisted they had gone to a "mountain preacher" and were already married! On investigating, we found this was true! The groom, just a young boy in his teens, whom we had not been able to meet, had come the night before, insisting they be married immediately. "I have to go right back to Ohio to my job. Besides, I ain't agoin' to dance down a church for nobody."

My first real tears at Morris Fork were visible all that afternoon.

Since there was no high school or even grade school available, in the early Morris Fork years, we decided the best way to take care of our teenagers would be to somehow try to send them away to school.

Scattered through the mountains were church schools of various denominations. But venturing away to school was a big problem, since our youngsters had never been away from their Morris Fork homes. After considerable persuasion, a few parents consented to the separation.

Mima Stamper was one of the first youngsters to go away. And such a sweet and lovable child she was. Mima came from a large family and needed much help. We watched and guided her in her high school years in the county. At the completion of these, she said, "Aunt Nola, I want to be a nurse." How excited and wonderfully happy this made us. We talked and we planned. Then, hoping to surprise me, Mima went to Lexington, where she made her application to a hospital. A bit later, she came to me,

106

telling me what she had done, and telling me also that she had failed the entrance test! We were both heartbroken.

I said, "Mima, I know there is a year's course of practical nursing you can take; let's try to find a place for you to do that." She consented, and I began the search. I could find no opportunity in Kentucky at the time, but a friend in Cincinnati located something there. Fresh plans were made. With the help of my friend and after much correspondence, all arrangements were finally completed for the fall term. Our friend was to meet us in Cincinnati and take Mima into her home until she could learn a bit about the city and find other suitable living quarters. There were no dorms for students in this program.

We worked practically all summer, getting what money we could for Mima's various needs. It was decided that I would go to Cincinnati to help her get started. She had to have uniforms and other clothing for the more sophisticated world that would surround her.

The afternoon before we were to go, Mima and her dad came to the community house. I could sense immediately that this was not my usual happy Mima. I feared the worst.

"Aunt Nola," Mima stammered, "I've decided not to go to Cincinnati."

"What?" I exclaimed.

"Her mammy and I decided we have to have her at home," her father said. "We can't let her go."

I tried to argue through my tears, but it was no use.

"I reckon," her father continued, "she can do just as good here. Her mammy isn't too well, and she needs her. And Mima ain't never been away from home; don't know how she'd get along."

All persuasion seemed useless. Mima had yielded to her parents' pleas.

I couldn't help but remember that one of our county agents had once said, "If I could give every mountain child a gift, I'd fill 'em chuck full of the 'I want to.'" Even though we'd worked and prayed so hard with and for Mima, it seemed that she didn't have enough of the "I want to."

I mustered my nerve and a bit of anger.

"Mima, you are one of my babies. I've loved you all your life and have wanted to help you 'be somebody.' But it seems you don't care. You won't take our help. Well, it's up to you. I can't force you to do what I'd like. But I'm telling you, *never* come back here asking for anything. I can't do any more for you. My friend in Cincinnati is looking for us tomorrow. She's expecting you to live with her. Now you and your dad will have to get to a phone in Hazard, some way. You'll have to call and tell her you're not coming. I can't do this for you." And with that, I ran tearfully across the yard.

All that day, my heart was heavy. One more failure . . . how could it happen?

Around midnight, there was a knock at the door. I heard someone calling. I opened the door and through the dim light I saw Mima and her father! "Aunt Nola," she exclaimed, hugging me. "I am going to Cincinnati; my mom and dad said I should. We'll be ready for the train in the morning."

Was I dreaming? No . . . just one more answered prayer!

Mima finished her year's training with honors. Several times her superintendent wrote me of her good work. "She is a very special nurse—many times patients ask for her. She is loving, sweet . . . and dependable."

A few years later, a note came from Mima. "Aunt Nola, don't be worried when I tell you I'm going to be married. I remember all the things you've told us about marriage . . . 'be sure to choose a clean, decent boy and be sure you really love him.' Well, I've done this. My boyfriend is going to be a Baptist minister. We want to be married in our Morris Fork church with you and Uncle Sam there. We want the wedding the last of next month."

Such hustling and such bustling. A Cincinnati wedding in our little Morris Fork church! Mima's mother, Ollie, was not well and needed much help to "prepare for the city folks." All of us went to work. We cleaned the church and helped put up new paper and curtains, in Mima's home . . . all just in time. Little Morris Fork was ready to welcome Cincinnati.

The wedding ceremony was lovely and went off just as planned. But Cathy Berger, who was very much with us as our Morris Fork teacher at the time, says she never *has* forgotten one particular moment that followed the wedding dinner:

"Swept up in the merriment, two of Mima's brothers, joined by some of their buddies, demanded a treat from the bridegroom and—in the best mountain tradition—announced as how they were going to ride him on a rail. When the boys attempted to seize him for the ride, a voice could be heard coming clearly from one of the doorways. It was that of Ollie Stamper. With shotgun aimed right at her eldest son, she told the boys to stop what they were up to . . . and they did!"

Mima went off with the happy groom later, continued her nursing and raised a quartet of radiant Christian youngsters.

Not much time was required for this idea of a Morris Fork wedding to "take." Even those who had gone to Ohio and Indiana or other far away places for work returned for this most important event to take place in the church. For the first time, the beauty and sacredness of the marriage vows really meant something, and these services became a very important part of our church and community life. All helped in preparation for them. The beautiful greens, plants, shrubs, and flowers from our hills furnished the lovely decorations, and a reception always followed the ceremony. In sunshine, the church garden was the setting. In inclement weather, the Sunday School room of the church itself made a festive reception parlor. Brides' and bridesmaids' dresses were almost always homemade— and the lovelier for it. Over and over, the bride would remind us how very much it all meant.

Not only our Morris Fork folks wanted all of this wedding activity. We were very much surprised to hear from a couple of our good Christian Endeavor friends in Louisville—"We are going to be married and want to come to Morris Fork. Can we have our wedding in the little church there?" Of course our answer was, "Yes, yes—come ahead."

The special wedding date was set. The couple chose to have a small wedding party of Morris Forkers, rather than to bring in Louisville folks. Neighbors and friends made ready. No city church could have boasted of more preparations for a wedding event.

The bride and groom-to-be arrived the day before the wedding, riding horseback from Buckhorn, where they had left their car—in pouring rain. I had been visiting different little schools for immunizations all day, but came home just in time to see the bedraggled and soaking wet "happy couple" riding up our little creek to the house. Never shall I forget the sight, the bride-to-be clutching a bouquet of flowers, all wet and drooping—trying to dismount from her restless, soaking wet horse.

"Well, here we are," were the first words I heard . . . spoken half cheerfully, half hopefully.

But a glowing fire in the living room fireplace soon revived the dampened spirits and clothing. A "wedding supper" was enjoyed, and happy final preparations for the big day were completed.

The wedding day itself was one of beautiful sunshine.

In June of 1980, as I was at work on this book, a note came from our Louisville bride and groom, with a little birthday greeting, plus $87.00 . . . $1.00 for each of my birthdays! And after all these 40 years!

I quite early learned that my saddle pockets were my riding drug store. But I discovered also that these pockets were not bottomless and that I would have to choose to carry only the absolute necessities.

For my confinement cases, I always packed a layette, and a mother's nightie. Alcohol, iodine, aspirin, boric acid, corn starch, morphine (which I never used), a cathartic, scissors, umbilical tape, Lysol, ergot, and a couple of extra sheets. Cough syrup was added to my list, and with quite a bit of malaria throughout the hills, I found quinine very helpful. It was useful, too, for other "fever cases." A supply of cotton and bandages, and some very early band-aids, found their place. For immunizations I carried my hypo, a small basin for sterilizing it, and several different serums and water.

Occasionally, when I knew there were to be children's immunizations, I'd "hide away" a bit of candy—some-times homemade—which helped to make these events more relaxed and less tearful. I learned that newspapers made a good pad for the bed, so these, covered with any-thing I could find as "clean cloths," were crammed into the bags in some way. There really was never enough room for all that I needed, so many times the "extra" had to be carried in front of the saddle on my lap.

One day in the Thirties, a large package arrived for me. Sure enough, it was a real nurse's bag—a black leath-er one! This was a wonderful gift from Kathryn "Casey" Conklin, our very dear Forest Hills friend, that made possible keeping my "baby things" separate from other supplies I needed for other cases. Soon it became quite common for the youngsters to call out, "Here comes Miss Nolie with a baby in her black bag!"

How well I remember the young mother with eclamp-sia, the first and only such case I had at Morris Fork!

I had been with this mother all night. All had seemed quite normal when the baby arrived about 5:00 a.m. After caring for the mother and the new babe, I went just up the road and home.

About ten o'clock, a scream came at the door, "Come quick, Bessie's dying!" Rushing to the house, I found her in convulsions. I was terror stricken. All seemed so helpless. Neighbors had come in and Sam was with me. "She will have to go to the hospital," I exclaimed. "Get to a phone quick and ask them to send an ambulance across the river!" There was a phone, by this time, in a home about three miles down the creek. A couple of men jumped on a mule with the message for the hospital.

Sam was busy getting more men to "fix a sled." We wrapped Bessie in quilts and put her on a cot. On the homemade sled, she was drawn by a mule about five miles down the creek, where the ambulance waited on the other side. Very quickly, again, the cot was taken from the sled and put this time on a homemade, man-paddled flat boat, which carried her safely across to the ambulance; then she was off to the small hospital in Hazard!

In three days the ordeal had ended; Bessie was back home, the little mother fine. Bessie's mother and I took care of the new little baby while she was gone—his grandmother nursed him! She had a young baby too, and was perfectly able to feed the two little ones. We had not yet heard of baby formula at Morris Fork.

Clinics became an early and important part of our Morris Fork program, after we found trachoma, typhoid, T.B., hookworm, and other various "worm disorders" so prevalent.

There was a trachoma clinic in Richmond, Kentucky. Since we had absolutely no facilities for this treatment, we made arrangements for our patients to go there. Whole families—mother, father, children—would go by wagon to Chavies, then via train to Richmond. This was an ordeal, but the treatments brought such relief and honest-to-goodness cures! Our people were so grateful and thankful for such an opportunity of actual healing.

We'd send tubercular patients to sanitariums in the state, occasionally as far away as Louisville. Specimens for worm conditions were sent to state labs, where treatment would be prescribed for home care.

Feeling a great need for a pediatrician, I got in touch with our good friend, Dr. Farra VanMeter in Lexington. Dr. VanMeter had treated, both surgically and medically, many patients we had taken to him. "I know just the fellow for you," he said, and it wasn't long before we were impressed with his praise of Dr. Harold Alexander, an outstanding Lexington pediatrician.

"Why, will he come?" I asked in amazement.

"Just ask him! And I'll tell you another good M.D. to have: Dr. Irvin Z. Kanner." Once more our earnest prayers were answered, though I must say almost beyond expectation.

Dr. VanMeter, Dr. Kanner and Dr. Alexander came as a volunteer trio to give us a Morris Fork clinic. This was before our electricity days so we had to use lanterns and kerosene lamps!

After the horseback ride from the train, the folks and all their instruments were unloaded, and everyone was welcomed into the community house. Mrs. VanMeter, who accompanied her husband, said, "I brought you a jar of mayonnaise; I didn't know if you could get it here." Unpacking, we found the mayonnaise in a box with the doctors' gowns. It had broken! There we were, with no washing machine to help clean up the mess.

But we managed—and went on to have a wonderful clinic for three days. Many treatments were given. Much good medical advice was offered, and some necessary plans made for those who were found to need surgery.

This was just the first of several Morris Fork clinics, all made possible by generous deeds of medical service.

In 1932 we were having a Sunday School County Convention over in Canoe, about fifteen miles by horseback from Morris Fork. Just before the afternoon session was to begin, Sam rode up to the little church there with two "guesties"—strangers he had found in Jackson. Chester and Margaret Ranck were on their honeymoon from Philadelphia. Always glad to greet visitors, we exchanged introductions. We were delighted with the offer of their friendly help, and asked if they might stay and help with the convention program. They seemed very happy to do so, and to find a place to stay.

Before long we discovered that Chester was a musician, with a strong and elegant tenor voice. How wonderful, we thought, that the Lord had sent this musician from Philadelphia to lead our little convention in music! And what a leader he proved to be!

Margaret had been a teacher in the Philadelphia schools. She and Chester had heard of the needs and opportunities in the Kentucky hills, and had decided to answer a call for Christian workers in southeastern Kentucky. Their decision had been made rather hastily, without much time for investigation. When they arrived at their designated station in Breathitt County, they were deeply disappointed. Things did not seem at all as advertised. Plans did not work out as expected, and soon they were dejectedly awaiting a train to take them back to Pennsylvania. Then Uncle Sam discovered them!

We had a glorious two days with our convention program and the Canoe folks. Both Margaret and Chester were thrilled. When we asked what they were going to do, back home, Chester said, "Well, we're not sure." Sam suggested that they come over to Morris Fork for a weekend. "We're canning peaches," I said, "and I'll be so happy to have some help."

So the Rancks came home with us to "take the night." They stayed two years, and gave generously of their talents to those early and important years at Morris Fork. They left in order to go to Owsley County where they opened Faith Community Center, which served for thirty-seven years the educational and religious needs in Ricetown, Bee Branch, Lucky Fork and Mistletoe. Margaret served as teacher for several of these isolated communities where there were no schools. Chester, an ordained minister, was pastor and builder, building churches where there were none. His fine voice filled our little church, and others, many times.

Although we had a new central school building by the mid-thirties, which replaced our community-built one that had burned in 1933, it was quite poorly equipped and had to be heated with a single stove. The coal fire had to be started and kept going all day with the children's help.

114

Sometimes there was very little heat, and lunches brought by the children were frozen in their buckets or paper pokes. This fact, combined with our continuing concern for better nutrition, dramatized the need for a sound school lunch program. This was a radical idea. Nothing of the sort had been suggested or even thought of by county officials or anyone else.

We had already organized a PTA in the community. Through discussion and planning with its membership, the school lunch program was "voted."

It was agreed that the children would bring canned fruits, vegetables, and milk from home whenever they could. Any milk was to be supplemented by a good quantity of goats' milk, from a large herd owned by one of our men. Needless to say, the youngsters were not informed that they were drinking this interesting blend!

The food was largely prepared by the children, before school, in the Community House living room. During the morning, it was cooked in our kitchen and carried to the school house to be served.

We knew that the children were eating corn bread for their three meals each day and wondered about introducing whole wheat bread for lunch. But how or where could we obtain it? There were no markets close-by that could supply it.

After much wondering and scheming, we contacted a bakery in Lexington, nearly a hundred miles away, that agreed to send a week's supply of fresh whole wheat bread by rail to Jackson, where good friends from Powell Hackney Wholesale Grocery would meet the train and carry the precious cargo as far as they could toward Morris Fork on their truck. Our men would meet the truck with a mule-driven wagon and bring the bread the last ten or so miles over our creek roads.

All our efforts were richly rewarded. The children loved the bread. Many times we ran out of it before the week was over, and our order would have to be increased.

All the after-lunch work was done by the children. We

had dishwashing, laundering, straightening up, scrubbing and silver committees, with duties rotated. Tea towels were laundered after each meal, and all the silverware was sorted and counted. Once a week. all the tables were carried outside to be scrubbed. These handmade tables were very heavy and roughly made. They required much tugging and pulling to get in and out. Scrubbing of the cement floor required that water be carried by bucketfuls and heated on a coal burning stove. All the dirty water then had to be swept out with brooms.

The Morris Fork lunch program was surely not a subsidized and modern program, but it may well have been one of the earliest ones in the nation. And again, the Church had led the way.

In the creeks and hollows of the Kentucky mountains were thousands of tired or soon-to-be tired women, women with potential, women whose wings had never been tried. They were hungry mentally, socially, spiritually. No "outsider" had ever come to them with sympathy or with any sort of encouragement. But now the church had come, offering the gospel of Jesus Christ, with his life more abundant for everyone . . . women included.

When Mrs. Harvey Murdoch came with her husband to Buckhorn in 1916, she sought out some of these women. The attempt was made to gather just the women together—to begin to talk with them and to plan in terms of "women's work opportunities." The first Women's Circle of the church was formed—and it was the very first in this whole mountain area as far as we knew.

Granny Blackman joined Mrs. Murdoch as an ardent helper in this venture. Word soon got around that mountain women were getting together to study the Bible and to learn something of what they could do for the Lord in His church and community—and, therefore, for each other.

What pride and joy we felt soon after, as "Women of the Church" at Morris Fork increased in wisdom and stature and in favor with God . . . and man. We organized a "Dorcas Society," which met weekly in the community

116

house. This was a time of fellowship with a devotional service, Bible Study, quilting, and much "talking over" of our needs and shared interests. We met weekly—not to hoe corn, but to work together and find our rightful place. These mountain women were receiving some identity and some constructive Christian training. Some real "liberating" was taking place long before E.R.A.!

Quilting was not new for these women; they had had to do this all their lives for their families. But when we began to talk about quilts for sale, this opened up a new and different sphere. No one had ever heard of such a thing! The quilting was beautiful with its tiny and lovely hand stitches. Patches and scraps of materials were obtained here and there. Very soon word of the pretty patterned and beautifully made quilts "got around." We began to fill orders for friends and church groups from "the outside."

Sometimes we discussed people and missions in other parts of the world and wondered what we could do to bring these folks some of the life more abundant that was now coming to us. We wanted to share . . . but what? A study of stewardship showed us we did have some things we could give. Chickens, eggs, corn, potatoes became part of God's Acre at Morris Fork. Money from the sale of these became our offerings.

Then we found coin cards. There was a slot for a dime a month. Could we find and save this and at the close of the year make our offering of at least a dollar apiece? Of course we could. And we did. As our coin cards were dedicated, we found we had several dollars for our first offering to help missions in other parts of our world.

We found we could do more than quilt and farm. We cooked, canned and shared in child care. And we made over clothes for needy children.

One of our most important days, a real highlight, was the time we entertained the Kentucky State Homemakers. We had organized our Morris Fork Homemakers with the Home Agent from the University Extension Service as often as she could get to us. We had also attended

Women of the church—around 1930. (left to right) Suzanne Morris, Clara Smith, Mary Morris, Sarah Turner, Nola VanderMeer, Martha Deaton, Lula Sandlin, Perilee Smith.

Homemaker meetings in Lexington. We were quite excited and thrilled with the Homemaker program, and someone suggested that the state Homemakers come to Morris Fork! Although it seemed impossible at first to attempt such an event, with hustling and bustling for several weeks we prepared ourselves for it.

The day of the grand occasion could not have been a more perfect one. All the summer beauty of our mountains was on full display. We served over 100 "guesties" chicken, dumplings, spoon bread, fresh garden salad, our luscious green beans, blackberry pie—all from our gardens. And—we Homemakers could hardly believe it—our own hubbies, dressed in fresh white aprons, served the tables! This was a history-making event, for these mountain men who were used to being first at the table, carefully tended and cared for by their good wives.

One day I asked about making choir gowns. "The young people in the choir need and want gowns. And I can get hold of some material," I said. After a few expressions of concern over such a challenge, we got some white muslin and set to work. Before long, and to the awe of

118

many, our choir appeared in the Sunday service in their homemade "choir shrouds," as the folks called them.

While we were making the "shrouds," several mothers talked quite a bit about music. "The young 'uns just love music; but they never had it in school or any time, until you came. They sure love to get together to practice." Somehow a thought came to me—piano lessons!

I asked if any of the children would like to play the piano. Of course they all thought they would. I said, "You know, some day I may not be here; and you'll need someone to play for church and Sunday School. Besides, you might want a piano at home if someone could play."

So a music class was started; and pretty soon there were six or eight pupils, including a couple of boys. With no instruments at home, these students had to come regularly to the community house for practice. And since there was no money to pay for lessons, they helped with our housekeeping . . . a new "maid" for each day!

It had been far from my remotest thoughts that I'd ever be a music teacher! I had no degree in music. In fact, I knew little about it. But along with all the other innovations of our "changing times" at Morris Fork, I thought music would help fill some vacant spots and create some ambition in lives that had been so very empty. I could help youngsters to read notes and to begin an appreciation of music. The class grew, and we were really getting quite a start. Then summer rolled around.

All of a sudden, the children stopped coming. Upon inquiry, I was told, "They got to work in the summertime . . . hoe corn and help take care o' the gardens. They can't just waste time playin' the piano." I was so let down—but no pleading could change this summer habit that slowed our music's progress. We simply had to resume in the fall.

One Sunday, Sam had to be away. A group of folks came asking me to preach in his stead. "Oh my me," I answered. "I've never preached in a church pulpit. Let's try to get someone else."

"We want you," they said. "You can do it. Please!"

Quickly, the thought came. This is my chance. So, I

said I'd try . . . just this one Sunday. Well, along with other things that came to mind that morning, I was led to say: "You know, the Bible has a lot to say about music and rejoicing in heaven. But I've never seen a word about hoeing corn. If all your children know is just hoeing corn, how will they be happy in heaven?" They never asked me to preach again!

In spite of my setback on the music front, our women were soon identified with Presbyterial and Synodical societies. We began to attend meetings all over the state and to hold statewide offices. On two different occasions, we sent delegates to join the five thousand from all over the world attending our International Presbyterian Women's Conference at Purdue University. What a thrill for our heretofore lonely and forgotten mountain women!

Just before Christmas—along in the Thirties—I learned that Dr. Robert Speer, former President of our Board of Foreign Missions, was coming to Louisville. Dr. Speer had labored in the mission fields and could preach the gospel as few of his day could. During all the years at Wooton and at Morris Fork, there had been no opportunity for concerts, lectures, or any such activity. We had been the ones constantly "giving out"; I was beginning to feel culturally starved. A chance to be in a "big meeting" to hear this dynamic leader just couldn't be missed.

"Oh, Sam," I said. "Dr. Speer is coming to Louisville—we must go hear him."

"That sounds good," he replied. "But Louisville is 200 miles away—doesn't look like we can make it."

But I just couldn't forget the event and quite frequently would bring it up. "Well," Sam finally said, "if we can make arrangements here, let's try to go." So, back in my head I began making plans.

"You know," I said, "I really don't have a dress for an occasion like this. I'll have to somehow get a new one." But there just were no shopping places, and we couldn't take time nor precious funds to go to Lexington. Looking through a catalogue one night, I was excited to find a semi made dress. "It's all done"—the ad proclaimed. "Simply add the bit of trimming that comes with it." "Just the thing," I said. When I showed it to Sam, he told me to go ahead and order it. The long satin dress came a few days before Christmas. It just needed trimming around the neck and waist. But I had to put it temporarily away— for at Christmas time, there was not a moment for any extras.

The Louisville trip was early in January. A couple of days before, I remembered the dress. Getting it out, I found several small velvet pieces to be appliqued around the neck and waist. "Oh, my," I groaned, "I'll never get it done."

That evening, I shared the challenge with Sam. We spread the dress on the floor. "Have any glue?" he asked, looking at the velvet pieces. I produced some and he promptly began gluing every little piece in place! I gasped again, and he said, "You wanted the dress ready, didn't you? Here it is." And there it was indeed.

At seven o'clock the next morning, Sam said, "Looks like we can't go. It's been snowing all night. The creeks are probably so icy the horses can't stand up on 'em." "Well," I said, "then let's walk. We just have to go."

"Walk to Chavies? Twenty miles?"

"It will be fun," I replied. We finished our packing, said goodbye to the couple who were to keep house for us, and began to walk the first 20 miles of our 200-mile journey to Louisville!

As we walked through the ice and snow, laughing, talking, and tugging our two suitcases, I came to a nice little path over the hill. "I'm going up here," I said, "to get out of the ice." But I soon came to the end of the path and yelled down to Sam, "This doesn't go any farther. What do I do now?"

"Sit down and slide," he said, "I'll catch you." As I came down the hill, I gained considerable momentum and couldn't keep from knocking Sam's legs out from under him. Both of us, and the suitcases, were suddenly sprawled all over the icy creek. We picked ourselves and our suitcases up and resumed our march. All that blessed day, we walked and walked, arriving at the station about fifteen minutes before train time at 7:00 p.m.

Flagging down the train, we hopped aboard, thankful for the warmth that came from a potbellied stove in the middle of the aisle. After catching our breath and getting our baggage settled, Sam said, "I'm going to take off my boots and put on my shoes." Off came the boots, but his feet were so swollen his shoes would not fit! In spite of this, we enjoyed the relaxation as we snatched a few little cat naps before getting into Lexington about midnight.

Lexington was having a snow storm too! Still Sam had no choice but to walk to the Phoenix Hotel in his bedroom slippers.

By train time next morning, everything was fine. We went on to Louisville, had time to get "dressed up" for the dinner meeting—and had a wonderful, wonderful evening. Dr. Speer never knew how his two ardent admirers came to his meeting!

Some six months later my handsomely decorated dress was sent to a cleaners. When it came back, by mail, a little note accompanied it. "We don't know what ever happened—all the applique pieces came off."

Sometime, somewhere, in my "evangelical training," I was taught to beware of any state university. Too dangerous were they and filled with "ungodly teachers." No young Christian would be safe within their walls!

On my way back home to Illinois for a bit of vacation, after a most hectic year at Morris Fork, I had to stop over in Lexington for the night. With some extra time the next morning, I found myself browsing about one of the fine department stores—right in the middle of an after-Christmas sale! I convinced myself that I really did need a new coat. With only a little help from an eager saleslady, I was persuaded to buy one.

When I got back to the hotel to ready myself for going on to Illinois, I found that I had spent too much of my traveling money for the coat and did not have enough to pay for my hotel bill and the rest of my trip. How careless

I had been! Trying to figure how I could get hold of a bit more cash, I remembered a minister who had visited us at Morris Fork. After some hesitation, I called him. Thinking of the many times my husband had endeavored to help someone in need, I reintroduced myself and told him of my predicament. I asked if I might use his name for identification in getting money from the hotel or bank. "I do not know who you are," came the reply. "You may be Mrs. VanderMeer, you may not. Besides, I have made it a rule never to loan money. I'm sorry. Good-bye." I was hardly able to hold back the tears.

Remembering another Lexington visitor whom we had had, I wondered if I dare make another call? "But he's at the University," I thought. "He'll never remember me." Time was getting short; I had to do something. With quaking heart, I found the number and called the University.

"Why, Mrs. VanderMeer," said the pleasant voice. "I am so glad to hear from you. I remember my good visit with you folks in the mountains—What a fine center you have there."

With a much uplifted heart, I explained my dilemma and confessed my reason for calling.

"Well," came the same cheery response, "We all get into tight places sometimes. You tell that man at the Phoenix desk to give you all the money you need; he can call me back. Glad you called. Have a good trip." This time the tears did come.

During all our years at Morris Fork, these "godless" University folks were behind us in all our programs— lending their skills, their good advice, whatever resources they could. They responded, whenever asked—and many times without being asked. It was their generous interest and help that "put over" the Community Fair which became such a part of our Morris Fork life.

Nothing that took place in those early years at Morris Fork equalled in excitement our preparations for each Christmas season. Early on, much that was happening to all of us together seemed to be summed up during those days and nights of decoration and caroling, when Heaven and nature sang.

In early December, groups of our menfolk would go into the hills for native greenery . . . holly, mistletoe and boughs. These would be brought to the church and community house, filling both with fragrances of the season. Huge wreaths were made and carefully placed all over the church. A beautiful tree would be put in the sanctuary and eventually lighted with honest-to-goodness candles! "Reminds me of the place where my Savior was born," one of our mothers murmured as she viewed the completed decoration.

A time that had been stained with terror and bloodshed, year upon year before, now knew the happy shouts of children as they hunted for Santa. There was a beautiful serenity to their faces as they sat around the great tree and heard the story of the Christ Child.

The hills that had known drunken shouts and vengeful firearms now heard the voices of carolers . . . as many as seventy strong. The weather of a particular Christmas did not matter. In mud, snow or bitter cold, we would often sing our way across the hills until nearly sunup.

When the time came for our annual letter in 1935, Sam composed it as though it had been written by a man named "Ed" to some of his friends, who knew of the old Morris Fork. In the letter, "Ed,"—like a Rip Van Winkle—told them about the many changes he noticed when he returned.

Two real and special guests in the Thirties helped to give us different but equally memorable Christmas times.

It was during a Presbyterian meeting that I first heard Nell Nix sing. She was a soloist during the services. Such a beautiful soprano! "Oh, if she could only come to Morris Fork," I thought, "how much that rich voice would mean for our Christmas music." But how could I meet her? Dare I ask such a person to come to our mountains? Mustering courage, I managed to introduce myself, telling her how grand her music had been, then asking if she could help with a Christmas program at Morris Fork. To my surprise, she said, "I'd love to come. Tell me more about Morris Fork." Almost too amazed to talk, I told her of our work. Immediately she said, "I'll let you know when I can come; I want to do it."

Soon after her arrival, Nell became a wonderful new friend. In all the weeks she was with us she gave beautifully of herself and her talents. I did discover that she was very careful of her appearance, always looking her best. And I wasn't too surprised, just before Christmas, when she asked, "Nola, where do you get your hair done?" In some perplexity, I responded, "What did you say?" She repeated her question, and I began to be astonished. She really meant it! I said, "You must have forgotten you are in the mountains—this isn't Mt. Sterling, Nell. We don't go anywhere to get our hair done. There's no place to go."

"Well," she exclaimed, "I ALWAYS have a fresh hairdo for Christmas. I've never done without one and I can't begin now." I tried to explain the impossibility of getting to a beauty salon. There was none nearer than Jackson, a sixty-mile roundtrip horseback ride away!

But Nell remained very much perturbed and upset. A couple of days later she announced, "I saw one of the boys running up and down the creek in a Ford. I asked him if he'd take us to Jackson and he said sure he would. If you'll go with me I'll pay for your getting your hair done, too."

I couldn't believe I'd heard her straight. Looking at her dubiously, I said, "Why, Nell, that's impossible. No one can drive to Jackson."

"Well, I'm going on Monday," she said, "and you can go too, if you want to."

With much trepidation, I said, "I've never been to a beauty salon in all the years I've been in the mountains, but if you can go, guess I can too."

By Monday morning, it was raining a bit. But about eight o'clock, sure enough, here came Edwin Morris and his Ford. I couldn't believe my eyes. With much astonishment himself, Sam helped us into the car. He had consented to keep house, going ahead with Christmas preparations while we had this "fling."

We splashed down the creek, over bumps and rocks, and through the water. It was pretty rough going, but not really bad until we came to the river, about six miles out of Morris Fork. The rain continued. "Say," said Edwin, "think you'd better get out and walk along here. The bank is very slippery, and I don't want us to slide into the river." So, out we got, into the mud and the rain, to walk for about a quarter of a mile.

When Edwin thought it was okay, we got back in the car and made the rest of the trip to Jackson with no more difficulty. Soon after arriving, we collapsed, with a sigh of relief, in the beauty salon chairs.

We had been under the dryer only about fifteen minutes when Edwin popped his head in the door of the beauty parlor and said, "Y'all ready to go? It's rainin' hard and we got to start back while we can still make it."

In dismay, I said, "Why, we can't go now, we have to get our hair finished, then I have to do a little shopping."

"Better hurry," he replied, "can't wait too long; don't want to get stuck in the mud on that river bank."

We did try to hurry. After our hair was finished, we ran over to the nearby A&P store for fruit. We got half a bushel of apples and half a bushel of oranges. Then I saw fresh oysters. When had I had fresh oysters last??? The more I looked at them, the hungrier I became for them. I asked the clerk if he could put them in ice for me, saying we'd be home in about four hours. He said he sure could. When he was done wrapping, I grabbed the box and the ice, packed the fruit in the back of the car, and off we went.

By this time, the rain, sure enough, was pouring down.

We didn't talk much as we drove homeward. Coming to the river bank again, Edwin said, "Better walk—this is too slippery to ride." Out we jumped, new hairdo and all, into the pouring rain. But very soon Edwin said, "You'd better get back in."

Cautiously, we took our seats, and even more cautiously, Edwin resumed driving, with the car slipping and sliding through the mud. We'd not gone more than a mile when he said again, "I'm sorry, but you'd better walk—I'm afraid I can't hold this car on the road—it's slipping everywhere."

Without a word, we got out again. It didn't seem to be raining quite so hard, so we tried to laugh and talk as we trudged along. After a bit, I didn't get any response from Nell. I turned around, but couldn't see her. My first awful thought was, "She's slipped into the river." Going back, I found her along the road, sitting in a mud puddle. As I helped her up and we stood there dripping wet, she said, "Whose idea was this—going to Jackson for a hairdo?"

Presently, the car came along and Edwin said it was safe to get in again. The next ten slippery miles were conquered very, very slowly. By the time we reached Long's Creek, it had become very dark, as well as cold and rainy. Suddenly, the Ford chugged to a halt. Try as he could, Edwin could not budge it. "The only thing now," he said, "is to get a team of mules to tow us home. You all stay here. I'll go up the creek and the first house I come to I'll get some mules and be back as soon as I can."

Once more Nell and I were practically speechless. We sat there in the pitch blackness of the night, shivering in our damp clothing, in a car that wouldn't move. After about an hour had passed, we saw a flashlight, heard some splashing, and, sure enough, there was Edwin with a mule team.

The team was hitched to the front of the car, and once again, under mule power this time, we were off! Up the creek we went, over the bumps, and through the endless mud. With the day's rain, the water in the creek had risen considerably. But this was not the first time the steadfast mules had prevailed.

It was around midnight when we saw the light of our Community Center house—all glowing and waiting for us! As we came to a halt and were trying to pull ourselves together to get out of the car, Nell said, "What's this all over the floor?"

"My goodness, my oysters," I said, and began gathering them up.

"What are you going to do?" Nell asked.

"Take them to the house and wash them—you don't think I'm going to throw them away after all this!" I replied.

And so we had one more adventure to add to those of a Morris Fork Christmas—beautiful, hectic and glorious as it always was.

We had fresh-washed oysters and un-done hairdos to show for Nell's "usual"—or was it *unusual*?—trip to the beauty parlor.

One of the earliest adventurers to call upon us from a distance was "Casey" Conklin. She became a part of our family from the time of her very first visit in 1935. Two years later, she resolved to join us for Christmas . . . our tenth at Morris Fork. Casey recalls it vividly:

> When I had written Sam to ask what I might send for gifts, Nola suggested a Christmas candle for each of the thirty families. We were delighted, made them ourselves from paraffin, and sent them down well before the Christmas rush.
>
> I arrived at Chavies after thoroughly enjoying all the friendly mountain folk on the train from Lexington. It started to snow, and I began to wonder about those last ten miles. The raccoon coat I had been loaned in New Jersey was most welcome, as were the long woolen trousers I wore. Trusting Silver and the man guide who led me, I was off in the blinding snow. But how peaceful it was—pitch dark—the sound of the horses and the icy snow hitting the dry leaves along the creek bed.
>
> For some distance there were no houses between Buckhorn and Morris Fork. But suddenly, in the dark, there was a candle in the window, and the first family along the creek came out to the door and greeted us. So THAT was the reason for the candles!! Each family along the creek had been given one, and been asked to light it when they heard us coming. Tears mixed with

snow on my face, and in spite of the cold, I felt like every holiday in the year rolled into one.

Then another, even more solemn thrill. Remember the legend that the animals knelt down in their sheds to celebrate Christ's birth? Many of the Morris Fork barns were very close to the creek, and the sounds of the contented cows, pigs and chickens made the story come alive. No one ever again can convince me that it is a story, and not the truth!

What a Christmas! I even played Mrs. Santa, with my great coat for stomach stuffing!! Some were amused that halfway through the "play party" the stuffing began to show between the buttons of the jacket. When one little girl received her package—she guessed that it was a doll. Before unwrapping it, she said, "I hope it's a purty one." I was mystified— weren't all dolls "purty?" In fact, I thought some of them were insipidly pretty. But when I asked Sam, he told me that probably she had only had dolls made of a corn husk, and that the store-bought dolls were the "purty" ones.

I cannot remember how many parties were planned for Morris Fork and out-stations that Christmas, nor how many times I "Skipped To My Lou" till exhaustion set in. Sam would egg the boys on to keep me skipping.

I will never forget the lighting of the Christmas tree in the church. It held dozens of real candles, unlit, and there was a pail of water close at hand in case of fire. Then two men of the church, with tapers, began to light them. One by one, the mountain men and women voiced their gratitude for the Christ, in ways we city folk never express it. How open-hearted and sincere they were, offering thanks for a husband, no longer running a still; gratitude for high school opportunities at a church school; and, most of all, joy that there *was* a church, that other Christians, many from far-off cities, cared enough to help. Most of all they uttered prayers of thanks for Uncle Sam and Aunt Nola, who had come to them by faith. How humbling, yet how uplifting it all was.

The Thirties and Morris Fork were brightened considerably by the faithful visits of our extension service County Agents.

The times—and especially the travels—being what they were, Henry Cravens and Conrad Feltner had little difficulty in recalling some of their deeply etched memories . . .

Henry recalled for me the first time he met Sam.

"I was in the County Agent's office in Jackson, soon after arriving there in February of 1931. In walked this tall, slender Dutchman with pleasant manners and a big smile. He made it seem mandatory that I come to Morris Fork, meet his men and young people and help start a 4-H Club."

Henry remembered that on one winter visit, "There were so many visitors, I had to sleep on the upstairs porch

Mary Louise Moore, home demonstration agent, and Henry Cravens, county extension agent, on one of their many helpful visits.

of the community house. It was a near zero night and I had to have so many covers over me I could hardly turn over."

On another—and apparently warmer—occasion, he spent the night with a Morris Fork family . . . "Long before daylight, I heard a chicken squawking. To my surprise, when I sat down to breakfast, we had hot biscuits, chicken and gravy!"

"I found Morris Fork to be more than a place, it was a spirit," Conrad Feltner said in a tape he sent to me:

When I went to Breathitt County in 1937, I found there were approximately thirty mission stations in the county . . . There were some eight or ten mission stations that were involved in all aspects of the community life: religious, social, health, economic, and educational. Of this group, Morris Fork Community Center stood out as the leader.

In those days, getting to Morris Fork was quite a task . . . a home demonstration agent and I arrived at the railway station in Jackson at 4:00 a.m. and took the train to Chavies. At Chavies, we were able to always find a car or truck that we could ride to Buckhorn. Prior to going we had written and made arrangements to secure two mules for the remainder of the trip . . . This six miles was over a mountain and up a creek.

On arriving . . . in the morning, we would have a 4-H Club meeting. After lunch the farmers would gather, and I would discuss agricultural recommendations with them, and the home agent would meet with the homemakers in the afternoon.

Three o'clock was the cutoff time to race back to Buckhorn to get the car or truck to Chavies and return to Jackson by train by 6:00 that evening. This, in good weather, was a very interesting trip. Rain, snow and all made it rather difficult.

I remember when I introduced hybrid seed corn to Breathitt County at the farmers' meeting when we met in the church . . . I explained drought resistance, root

131

systems . . . increased yield. When I finished, Sam indicated, "Well, I think this is a good thing. I'll be going to Jackson . . . let's all try a little o' this, maybe a quart of seed each. I'll be glad to pick it up and we'll share."

I understood that the following Sunday, after we discussed hybrid corn, he worked this into his sermon in a very interesting way so that everyone there had some information relative to hybrid corn.

Another example that impressed me no end was what happened when we selected Warren G. Harding Riley to be one of the five boys to attend 4-H week at the University of Kentucky. It was around 1,500 members at that time . . . It was quite an honor to be chosen to represent our group at the University for a week. After discussing the different ones over the county, the home agent and I agreed on offering this opportunity to Warren. I wrote him a letter and congratulated him and asked him to come down on the train on a certain Sunday. I said I would meet him at Quicksand at the tunnel and that he would stay over with us that evening and then we would leave the next day for Lexington and 4-H week.

I got a very interesting letter back from Warren. He was simply thrilled at having had this opportunity, but in closing said he would be unable to go because he had to stay and work in the corn with his father.

I was very disappointed, but in the next mail I received a letter from Sam saying "Meet the train. Warren will be there.—Sam and Nola."

It was some months later that I found out that Sam had visited the home [I had sent him a carbon copy of the letter] after the letter'd been written by Warren . . . had told the family that this was too good an opportunity for Warren to miss, and for Mrs. Riley to get his clothes washed . . . he'd see that he [Warren] got over to Chavies to catch the train.

When the father indicated he needed Warren to work in the corn, Sam said, "Monday mornin' I'll be up here with my hoe.'' And that was Sam, always there to help, and nothin' was too menial or too unimportant that would help some individual, or the community, or the family . . .

One of the things that always impressed me about Sam and Nola was that they always set standards in everything that they did, not too far above the community, but challenging enough that it caused the young people and adults to want to do better . . .

I worked in Breathitt County eight years and, following that experience, went to Owen County for eight years as county agent. Then I moved to Lexington to the state 4-H office. It was after I arrived that we were able to secure the services of Uncle Sam to come to 4-H week each year and to conduct the vespers for the some 1,500 youths from all over Kentucky who were in attendance . . . he always had a private room in the dorm, and you could go up late at night and there would always be some of the boys talking to him about their personal problems, ambitions, and goals. And it was really interesting to see the tremendous impact he had on this group of young people for such a short period of time that they were exposed to his work.

Some three or four years after he started doing this for us, we had a new state 4-H leader, who decided that we should have someone else rather than Uncle Sam. The staff was very much upset about this. And, as it turned out, so were the young people.

. . . During 4-H week they themselves prepared a petition, circulated it and got hundreds of youths, leaders and agents to sign, requesting Uncle Sam be brought back the following year.

. . . Uncle Sam returned the following year and continued in this capacity until he was forced to quit because of sickness.

A personal example of the way that Uncle Sam got close to young people during 4-H week was my own daughter. Merritt's only contact with Uncle Sam was

133

through hearing me talk about him and the brief encounter she had with him during 4-H week. But after she finished college, and was making preparations to get married, she was home one weekend and said, "I want you to drive me over to Morris Fork. I want to see Uncle Sam. I want to see if he will perform the marriage ceremony."

When we arrived, she greeted Uncle Sam and said that she would like for him to marry her. He said, "Well, Honey, I'd just love to but I'm already married to Aunt Nola!"

Conrad Feltner's recall of Warren Riley's experience has reminded me of something else that happened, another 4-H footnote.

As our young Ray Cornett was about to leave to represent our club one year in Lexington, I gave him a postcard addressed to his folks. "After you are settled," I told him, "write a little note on this and put it in the mail so your Mom will know you are okay."

The days of the conference week slipped by—with no word from Ray. "We know he is alright," we told his anxious parents. "If anything is wrong, we'll hear from the University."

Finally Saturday arrived—and so, safely, did Ray. He was "full up" of good times and started to tell us about them. All of a sudden, he stopped and drew something from his pocket. "Oh, yes," he said. "Here's your card! I kept it for you."

"The Tired Country" did not really smile until the sameness of every day—that had made for the sameness of so many years—changed . . . changed with the coming of new traditions, of work and play, of learning and worship, of welcoming and being welcomed.

It wasn't enough to have windows to open in our cabins and houses. We needed to use our doors. We wanted the "door" to Morris Fork itself like the door of our little brown church, to be a welcoming door. And just as the door of the church opened to a renewal of life

134

beyond it we wanted the "door" of Morris Fork to be open to knowledge and friendship from the world beyond.

We wanted our creek bed at first—and then our own little hand cut road itself—to be a well travelled path. Of all the activities and traditions that used the "door" of Morris Fork and kept our path well worn, none did so more than those of the parties and special occasions of each year, and the longer commitments of our summer camps and our Community Fair. Because of them especially, the sameness of days vanished . . . and "the tired country" smiled.

Before our arrival, there never had been a time when attempted parties hadn't ended in a drunken brawl. Our folks were really starved for recreation: the sort that would re-create their hungry souls and bodies. In our early days, we had some difficulties of our own with what we planned. We discovered it was necessary to have "guards" at the doors and even around the building, to keep "whiskey carriers" away. More than once, drunken men and boys would have to be taken off the grounds and fights would have to be stopped.

Some folks thought we should not attempt the parties, but Sam said, "The devil is trying to hang on; he wants us to give up everything to him. Let's not do it!" And, little by little, even the troublemakers realized that this was not a place for them. They grew weary in the fight, and before long folks were saying, "You know, we had a party last night and there wasn't a single drunk there; we didn't have any trouble." After our big new country schoolhouse was constructed in the early Thirties, it became a great asset, for we had a very large room where we could "play." And our weekly Friday night parties became so well known, young people would come from a distance.

We learned some of the old English folk games . . . "Skip to My Lou," "In and Out the Window" and others. The only accompaniment for these was our own singing. Nine o'clock came all too soon. "One more game, please, Uncle Sam, just one more," was the plea many times. After always obliging, Uncle Sam would have everyone sing a hymn and join hands in a circle of closing prayer. Then, with kerosene lanterns swinging gently against the darkness, all could be seen making their way home.

Through the years, as drunkenness disappeared and it was safe to have "night doings," pie and box suppers became popular. Pies were baked, or box suppers prepared, and these were auctioned off. This became quite a social event enjoyed by all. The buyer was not supposed to know whose supper or pie he was buying. After paying for the "tidbit," he was expected to see the girl home.

Extension services from Berea College gave us much help and inspiration in those days of developing our recreation program. Teachers from Berea came to help our teachers; these crafts experts and recreational specialists had considerable impact.

As we planned for one of the recreational leaders to come for a two week "seminar," one of our men said: "Now, Uncle Sam, you are doing a lot of new things here, things we've never heard of, and we've tried to follow—to go along with you. We want to help all we can, but I just don't see any sense in getting a man in here to teach us how to play! What we need is work—not play." After a little more gentle persuasion and talking things out, Jim decided it might not be so wrong to learn a bit more about having a good time in the right sort of way. So Dick Chase from Berea came, to "play" with us. At the end of his visit, Jim said, "Well, this has been such a good time! You've learned us many things. Wish you'd stay longer, but if you have to go—you can ride my mule to the railroad station."

The only problem that remained now was the "supply and demand" one—how to provide all the recreation we had encouraged folks to enjoy. The holidays of our calendar seemed to take care of this.

New Year's Day was elected as the day for doing something special for parents and other older folks. Older

136

children were asked to take care of the younger ones so "Mommie" didn't even have to have "the least one" with her. News soon spread that there was to be an "old people's party." The fun began with table games before dinner. For dinner itself, everyone brought chicken, dumplings, beans, fresh cabbage that had been "holed away" for the winter, plenty of cakes, apples, blackberry pies and good corn bread.

After dinner, there were more games and much singing. The afternoon was closed with a New Year's service of hymns and prayers of reconsecration for the things of God, and a better life in the coming year.

Since love of the Christ was being spread abroad, why not bring special emphasis on love for each other into our hearts and homes. Valentine's Day became a fun time when our families came together just to play and "talk." We would all make hats of paper plates—the young people in competition with their parents! And special prayers would always be included—for a deeper, growing love in and amongst our families, our neighbors—and everybody!

At Easter time, the message of the sacrifice of Christ and the Risen, Living Lord became real.

The young people's choir would work weeks with special Easter music. Sometimes this was a cantata of the Resurrection. At other times, there would be a medley of the old Easter hymns combined to tell the Resurrection story. Eventually, we learned a modified version of the Hallelujah Chorus! What a thrilling achievement this was.

On the day before Easter, we would have an Easter egg hunt for our children . . . of all ages.

On Easter Sunday, there was always a processional beginning out of doors and moving down the church aisle into the choir loft . . . a processional of our young people, in maroon choir robes, singing jubilantly, "Hallelujah, He is Risen." There was neither a shot nor a drunken yell. Morris Fork rejoiced.

It is impossible to describe the rustic beauty of our little church on Easter morning. The beautiful, native wild flowers, the greens, the flower decorated cross, the church bell ringing out the Easter message. High on the hill, above the church, a cross had been placed by our young people in remembrance of Him who had died—and risen —for us.

One week, just before Easter, Sam had to ride "to the city" for a meeting. "What can I bring you?" he asked, as he left.

"Nothing special," I repled, "just hurry back."

In a couple of days, he returned. I couldn't believe my eyes as he rode into the yard. In front of the saddle, in his arms, was the most beautiful Easter lily! All the way from Lexington, a hundred miles away . . . he had carried it to Chavies on the train, and the rest of the way, some thirteen miles, he and faithful "Hi O Silver" had trotted it to Morris Fork. Such a living armful!

For several years, Chester Ranck made a very special contribution to our Holy Week. He would ride his mule the eight miles from Buffalo to spend Wednesday, Thursday and Friday nights with us, offering, with his fine voice, wonderful programs of Easter music on each of them.

On Easter Day in 1961, the first sunrise service was held atop the new Buckhorn Dam. The service, which has become another tradition of special meaning to folks in Breathitt and Perry Counties—and beyond—had been a dream of Sam's from the time he had first realized what a dramatic sunrise setting the dam would provide. On the first Easter after Sam's passing in 1975, I was invited to offer a prayer in the fifteenth anniversary service. Sam was so much with us that morning.

Memorial Day was given to graveside services. As many graves as possible were visited and decorated, with a prayer and hymn offered at each. So many requests came for visitations that this Sunday afternoon tradition eventually grew into a Friday and Saturday one as well.

In the very early years in our mountains, circuit riders

138

would find some of the isolated settlements such as that which became Morris Fork. Perhaps once a year they would spend a weekend in one of these. Their services developed into "graveyard meetings." At the actual time of a death, there was, more often than not, no minister available for a service. So "services" would be held up until a minister did come.

Folks would climb the rough, rocky, and often muddy paths that led to the graves. Often these cemeteries might be close together, some families having them on their own farms. Eventually, such services became annual, with the same "funeral service" being held over and over for those who had died the past year. This resulted in memorial services being conducted all through the summer with many participating ministers, as more and more local men felt a "calling" and wanted to preach. There were of course no conflicts in those communities without a church. But at Morris Fork, if the folks attended these gatherings, our regular church practices would suffer. The problem was solved with Sam's devoted and tireless cemetery visitations, which were scheduled so as not to conflict or compete with our regular worship.

On the first Fourth of July Sam spent in the mountains, he hoed corn all day under the hot sun, alongside Buckhorn boys and girls. "How terrible," he thought, "no recognition of our nation's birthday, and this amongst some of our 'truest' Americans." When he returned to make Morris Fork his home, he vowed that the Fourth of July would become a very special day. His Dutch American patriotism and the spirit of "Mother Rose" went into that resolve.

Over the years, we invited folks to an all day gathering, that included a big community dinner. We would salute our Christian and American flags and sing patriotic hymns with considerable gusto. Annual speakers soon were added, and their messages gave further focus and outreach to our celebrations. Food, games and fellowship

—with our ever widening circle of friends—would go on well into the evening.

Our Halloweens were well supplied with "spooky" games, and always featured a ghost march around the Community House grounds and some good ghost tales around our bonfire. There was no "trick or treat," but there was generally a bountiful supply of toasted marshmallows!

It was so hard for us to believe that Thanksgiving—if only as a harvest celebration—had never been known. But, as with our other observances, we simply "built" it completely.

For our Thanksgiving service, the church was always decorated abundantly with pumpkins, onions, squash, cornstalks and jars of sorghum—God's gifts to our gardens.

Our Young People's Choir provided special music—including the great Dutch hymn "We Gather Together." There would be testimonies of thankfulness from folks, recalling their own family heritage as well as our national one.

After the service, Uncle Sam would announce, "There are turkeys all around here. Who wants to go on a turkey hunt?" Sure enough, perched in the trees and concealed around the grounds were paper turkeys he had made personally and hidden. Such a scramble of our children and some of our oldsters. The grand prize? A couple of brand new pencils for the most turkeys found. Then a great potluck community dinner!

A good ball game would round out a host of games. And the call "Uncle Sam, a party tonight?" would be heard—and acceded to! Everyone participated willingly in all the clean-up from such a big day.

The meaning of Christmas to Morris Fork—and of a Morris Fork Christmas to friends from far beyond—is told in several different corners of this little book, so I will

140

not recall it here. By its appearance, of course, in so many places, it is obvious that it was of deep importance to our lives.

Christmas came but once a year at Morris Fork, just as elsewhere, but it surely lasted throughout each year for us.

The annual Birthday Party was kind of a bonus holiday for all. The custom had grown in our Sunday School program for a birthday offering to be brought as birthdays came around—a penny for each year.

Someone said it would be nice to have community birthday parties, so, instead of one each month, we had one a year each summer! Twelve tables were set-up in the yard— they were gaily decorated according to the month —and each person found his table—this was another "potluck dinnertime" when everyone brought food. It was a time of much merry singing around the tables—a huge lighted birthday cake—and everybody wished everybody a happy birthday and "good new year."

Perhaps no single tradition better symbolized the change that had come over Morris Fork in our first decade of work and prayer together than the daily ringing of our outside prayer bell. It became our Angelus.

As the bell was rung, near day's end, its toll was heard up and down the creek. For a few moments, a hush descended . . . work and conversation stopped . . . heads bowed in prayer.

On hearing about this daily moment that had become very special to us, and to those who visited us, Dr. Charles Zarbaugh of the Forest Hills Church in Newark penned some verses that seemed to even add to its meaning to all of us. They close this book.

Two of our strongest new traditions combined work, worship and well-being in very special ways. Each welcomed resources beyond as well as within our Kentucky corner. The first was our "work camp."

Not very many years after our marriage, churches that

had become acquainted with Morris Fork asked if it might be possible for some of their young people to come to help. "We want to be better acquainted with missions and our missionaries. We feel we can help you, and that you can help us. Can we send some of our young people for a week, or perhaps two weeks?"

This posed a new project for us, and something of a problem. We were not really set up to take care of groups; we had only our community house in which we lived and carried on the many community activities. But we could see that these young people might be a very valuable asset to our work, and to the programs of our contributing churches. Surely there were many "jobs" for an interested enthusiastic group.

Our first work camp group was provided by our ever faithful Forest Hills friends. They traveled as far as they could by car, then into Morris Fork, some fifteen miles, by a mule-drawn jolt wagon. What an experience for these rather privileged Newark youngsters! But what a happy, enthusiastic bunch they were—living the primitive life of the early settlers. We made room for them in the community house, giving a couple of bedrooms to the girls; leaving the boys to spread their sleeping bags on the first floor of the community room. We took all of them in around our dining table—"Aunt Nola" cooking for all!

Yearly thereafter, all through the summer, different work groups came from many different city churches. There were so many jobs they were able to do—painting, carpentering, digging wells and ditches, working in the gardens—along with helping with Bible Schools, Sunday Schools and church services. Of course they soon outgrew the room in the community house, so a log cabin was built—our "Campers' Cabin." Then, the hayloft of the barn was converted to a boys' dorm, and after a few years, it was found more convenient for the young people to do their own cooking.

The hundreds of young folks who came to work, play and worship through the years gave us a warm friendship —not only with themselves, but with churches throughout the United States. Letters from the pastors of these churches told of the deeper Christian life and impact of these young people in their homes and churches.

It didn't take long for us to become a part of the County Agricultural program once we discovered 4-H camps and conferences that were going on. Anxious to be a successful part of these opportunities, we planned carefully for our first camp trip with several of our children. "We'll have to ride to Buckhorn," said Uncle Sam, "go on to Chavies, and then take the train to Jackson. We'll have to walk from Jackson to Quicksand; that's about three miles, so we'll leave here about four o'clock in the morning."

At 2:00 a.m. the morning of the trip, a knock came on the door. There stood two campers! "My goodness," said Sam, "It's not time to go yet. Go home and come back in a couple of hours."

Three o'clock came . . . and another knock. "We're ready to go, Uncle Sam," they said, "and hit's raining."

"Well," Sam said, "Guess we might as well go, if it isn't raining too hard, so come in and get dry."

For this first camp, the children had to bring live chickens and whatever vegetables they could from their gardens, as well as their bedding and clothes. With all this packed on the mules and horses, they took off, in the rain, for the six-mile ride to Buckhorn. There they got a truck to take them over the gravel road to the railroad stop at Chavies. After they and all their supplies were on board, the excitement of the train ride commenced and went on for the entire twenty miles to Jackson. Then came the three-mile trek, with all the equipment, up the tracks to Quicksand!

Such a week of fun and fellowship, in the "outside" world, followed. On the return journey, one of the girls, who was riding in the train alongside Sam, looked up at him and said, "Uncle Sam, the Lord sure is mighty good to us, isn't He?"

With our 4-H Clubs and Homemakers and Men's Clubs all thriving, Sam suggested we undertake a community fair. "It will be good to see what everybody is doing—to compare our products."

"Alright," the folks said, "we don't know much about it, but we'll try."

A few came for the first fair—but without exhibits. "We don't have stuff that's good enough to show other folks," they said. "We just fix it for ourselves. It's just our livin'."

So the first fair passed in Morris Fork . . . something of a disappointment. But the bit of my own canning I displayed did seem to offer a ray of hope. At least the folks took note of it and talked about how nice everything looked. Undaunted, Sam said, "We'll have a good fair next year; wait and see, everybody will help."

And Sam was right. The next year we did indeed have a good fair . . . and the next year, and the next and all the nexts. Through the years, our fairs became one of the major events and parts of our community life. They became another new tradition, filling days as well as shelves that had been empty before.

During those first good but hard years at Morris Fork, I had experienced two miscarriages, which were largely the consequence of too much horseback riding to safely deliver other babies! Many times I would have to be on the job without rest for as long as thirty-six hours. I finally heeded my doctor's advice and went off to the restful corner of my parents' home in Illinois, where our son Billy arrived safely in the spring of 1933. We were exultantly happy—and the same again in 1937 when, after yet another miscarriage, we adopted a sweet baby girl who became our Mary Elizabeth.

In 1938 a call came asking us to "fill in" for a year or so at our Presbyterian Farm School (now Warren Wilson College) in North Carolina. With the very willing agreement of John and Lillian Abnett, who were our "right hand folks," and the approval of our supporting Forest

144

Hills Church in New Jersey, we decided to accept the opportunity. After ten years "a-buildin'" at Morris Fork, we felt a need for restful change and refreshment. Some part of our fatigue had come from frustrations of wanting to move ahead more rapidly; we had gotten a little tired in "the tired country."

At the Farm School, Sam's duties were mainly teaching ones. Of course, whenever he worked with young people, a good amount of counseling was inevitable. Since the enrollment was of boys only, with much of their study in agriculture, he was very much at home.

What a shock to be so much back in "civilization," with its electricity, cars, blacktop roads, refrigeration, telephones, and all those trimmin's. And there was no horseback riding!

And yet, even before year's end, we had a big case of Morris Fork homesickness—a sure sign we were ready to return and press forward.

I could not help but feel pleased over the growth in our community spirit for sharing as I looked back on it from the midst of an experience that took place at the Farm School. Although it was an unhappy ripple in an otherwise good year, it made me appreciate that command support is vital—even to a missionary effort.

Soon after arriving, the school dietician was given a leave of absence. I was asked, therefore, to help in the kitchen and dining room. I welcomed this, for I loved to "experiment" with cooking and to be around the boys as we prepared meals.

One day the boys asked especially for ice cream. "We make it," they said, "but we have to save the cream." Since our good herd of cows was milked twice a day, I said, "It won't take long to save the cream; we'll keep it in the refrig until there is enough."

For several days, we skimmed the good cream from the milk. Coming into the kitchen one morning, I said, "We should have enough cream; let's make our ice cream today." But on going to the refrig, I could find no cream, not even a container. "Why, where is our cream?" I exclaimed. "Let's look around," one of the boys said. He went to the cereal shelf. "Just as I thought," he said, "cereal's gone too." He led me outdoors to a half hidden spot—there were empty cereal boxes. "The kids have been eating it on the sly with all our cream."

I went to the Dean about it, but he said they were used to that and that the boys had always done it. "But what about when they take food we've been saving for a special meal?" "Well," he replied, "there's not much we can do—they've always done it." To me it was plain stealing. I felt something should be done about it, since it apparently had happened a good many times.

Then, a bright idea came to me. "I'll fix 'em," I said to myself. So I made a batch of candy, putting ipecac in it. It is, of course, a harmless drug used when a substance needs to be removed from the stomach. It simply causes . . . nausea. Sure enough, the next morning several boys came to the infirmary, where I had my office. They said they were very sick, and had been vomiting. I quickly took care of that, asking their names and scurrying off to the Dean's office. "Well, I have found our thieves. I know exactly who is stealing things from the kitchen."

"What do you mean?" he asked.

Then I told my story. I'll never forget how his eyes stared right through me. Rather angrily, he said, "What a thing you have done—don't ever try that again. This is the only home these boys have while here. They would get into their mother's icebox at home, so we'll let them do it here." I could not believe what I had heard.

7
The Forties

Touched by War and Peace

Although much of our day-to-day life at Morris Fork was not changed or affected by the coming of World War II, it did reach into our homes. As before, many of our young men went to Lexington to enlist. For a few, their return was an honored but sad one to the little cemeteries of our hills.

Mary Brewer, whose father-in-law Albert had brought me into Wooton in his wagon in the midst of another terrible war, wrote some lovely memorial verses that are so apt for all those mountain boys who died so far from home:

He shall not play upon the hill again
In winter snows and gentle summer sun.
Or come with slender hands turned dark with stain

From walnut hulls, and tired when day is done.
Nor shall he sit with us at Sunday School,
His golden head bowed low with thoughts that run . . .

A boy's thoughts, of hills, of fishing pools,
Of horses at the plows . . .

In Sam's letter telling of our Christmas in 1942, there was much that spoke of how the war had come into our

147

A very peaceful moment in the Forties. Emma Reeverts and friend—joined by Bill and Mary Elizabeth—pose on their mounts outside the Community House. The pup in the road is "Lexie," a stray we rescued in Lexington.

lives . . . and of how deeply we had been touched also by the death of one of our little ones.

The Church was lovely; a huge holly wreath was hung around the beautiful service flag with its nineteen blue stars and one gold star. Holly branches were over the windows, tall red candles sent forth a glad Christmas light, and a wondrous tree, towering to the rafters and laden with shining tinsel and ornaments, made little eyes grow big with wonder. But there were no happy greetings or pleasantries—sadness seemed to be in the air, and as the church bell began to ring, the reason for the sadness became apparent. Four men came in carrying a casket in which lay the body of one of our school girls who had been burned to death. She had toppled from her little chair into a blazing fireplace. The casket was placed under the spreading branches of the tree—seeming terribly out of place at first and we wondered how we could conduct a funeral service in such a setting. But we did, and it turned out to be a wonderful experience. The family had requested that we have our usual Christmas Day service and that we light the tree because the little girl had always enjoyed that so much. The church was filled, and we sang the lovely carols. A Christmas message was brought reminding us that we needed to go beyond the decorations of Christmas to the Christ, Himself, and worship. A visiting pastor reminded us that at the first Christmas there was the gift of Myrrh, symbolizing sorrow and bitterness, but there was also gold and frankincense. Then a pure white candle was lighted for the child who had gone Home, candles for our men in the Armed Forces, candles for our friends in Newark, Ashland, Newport, Cincinnati, Haledon, Paterson, Columbus, New York, Pennsylvania, Illinois, Rhode Island, and so many other places, until the tree was ablaze with lights. We were experiencing the real meaning of Christmas—"Emmanuel—God Is With Us"—a God who is ever present and all sufficient—in times of sorrow as well as times of joy. The sadness was lifted and somehow it seemed that there was a manger under the tree instead of a casket. We realized that because a Babe had been born in a manger, this child could now have her first Christmas in Heaven and join in the "Glory to God in the Highest." Outside the rain had increased and we were loathe to leave the beauty and light and warmth for the chill, the mud and the water. [I remember so vividly to this day the children gathered about the tree singing "Jesus Loves Me." In spite of our tears, we rejoiced that because a Savior was born, she would live again. N.V.] We placed the Christmas dolly in Vesta Ellen's arms, and then began to make our way up the Creek with her little handmade casket. A rough log mule team carried it to the foot of the mountain, then the men and boys took turns bearing it to the top.

Someone had said, "The divine plan for our different lives is like a mosaic, each piece needed to make a whole . . . " To us Christmas has been like a mosaic —made up of unusual pieces and put together under strange circumstances. Here are some of the pieces: A month of rehearsals for a glorious Christmas Cantata: eleven piano pupils practicing every day; two children severely burned at fireplaces—making many trips necessary for Nola; the hauling in of mail via muleback, sled and wagon; countless folks dropping in for clothing and counsel; call for Nola for a baby case way up on Burton Fork when creeks were raging torrents; a telegram stating that one of our finest young men had been killed in action on the African Front; visits to the home of the heartbroken parents; his funeral service; the erecting of a cross in the Memory Garden in his honor; the daily routine of country life, milking, churning, bread making; and all to the tune of the worst weather we have ever had in December! Now, all these pieces put together make the mosaic of our Christmas. The pattern is strange but hearts have been comforted, children made glad and there is peace in our hearts and good will towards men.

Sam was into his forties when the hostilities began. He endeavored to spread himself as effectively as he could over the church and community activities which were by then so numerous and which had come to depend in part on the help of our young men. But it was inevitable that

150

the war would finally reach his rather restless patriotism. When it did, the call came as an invitation to serve a large church program in Wilmington, North Carolina, in an area surrounded by military installations and defense industry. It was a situation in which Sam's energies would be fully tapped.

I can't recall Sam's decision to go to Wilmington in 1944 without remembering here a letter that came to us many years later. It was from his brother "Jake," and was a reminder of a very special anniversary.

March 25, 1971

Dear Brother and Sister,
Thought you might have forgotten that the above date is a very important one in our family history. It was on this date in 1903 that for the first time we had a glimpse of the Statue of Liberty in New York Harbor. Then the S. S. *Noordam* brought us to the docks at Hoboken, N. J.

As strangers, we came into a strange land, yet a land of marvelous opportunity. Truly a land flowing with milk and honey, compared to Holland in those days. Well do I remember the first night at the William Steigenga home, when five of us children were placed in one bed, lying crosswise. Then a day or so later we moved into our home on Wood Street, the Bunkerhill section of Paterson . . .

As we reflect today, our family has produced men and women of whom we can justly be proud. Not too many perhaps had the opportunity of going on to schools of higher learning, but most of them were endowed with a great deal of common sense, and were not afraid to roll up their sleeves and work. And to a large extent is not this a good cross section of what has made this great land of ours what it is today?

American patriotism was in the marrow of the strong Dutch bones of the VanderMeers. I had become aware of this when Sam first took me as his bride to meet them all in New Jersey. To Sam, the call to serve in Wilmington was one from God and country.

151

We decided that it would be good for Billy to go along to be near his dad and to experience what would certainly be an interesting year. How interesting it was for Sam shines through a letter he wrote back home to the *Jackson Times*. The letter afforded him the chance to tell his many friends why he had decided to go to Wilmington and just what he was up to. In the course of doing so, he said:

"Geographically, Wilmington, N. C. is about 600 miles from Morris Fork, Ky., but in my heart the distance seems very small. I guess it is because my heart is in the hills of Kentucky, even though my bodily presence is far removed . . .

"Just before leaving Morris Fork one of the men of the community said to me, 'Sam, do you have to go to Wilmington?' And I said, 'Well, did Paul have to go to Macedonia?' and this seemed to satisfy him. Since coming to Wilmington there have been many evidences that God has led me here and I feel sure that the time spent here will be made to count for the glory of God."

As Assistant Minister of the First Presbyterian Church of Wilmington, Sam reached out to the many servicemen and shipyard workers in that coastal area. He even managed to organize a new outlying congregation which, with the resources and interest of two other groups, grew to be self-supporting.

By the time Sam and Billy left Wilmington to rejoin us (Sam's niece, Anne DeBlock, and our daughter, Mary Elizabeth, had helped me to carry on at Morris Fork), his impact on one family had become so deep that their friendship would come to have special meaning to Morris Fork and, later, to another even more remote corner of the world.

Dr. "Sandy" Marks and his wife Kitty had welcomed Sam warmly into their home. They journeyed to Morris Fork at the end of the war and brought their entire household for a second visit later. On each of these occasions, not only the arms but the jaws of Morris Fork were opened to Dr. Marks! Impressed by Sam with our great need for dental care, he had volunteered to provide as much as he could during this, his "vacation" time.

But extracting permission to have our first dentist was like pulling teeth! Sandy had written the Kentucky Dental Association and they had replied that he couldn't come, since there was no reciprocity between North Carolina and Kentucky.

"Reciprocity, nothing!" I wrote him. "We need you, you are all ready to come, so don't pay any attention to them. There is no dentist anywhere from whom you'll be 'stealing trade;' they don't pay any attention to us!"

But Dr. Marks wrote back saying that if this were a Kentucky law, he'd have to obey. If they wouldn't let him in, he couldn't come.

We were too flabbergasted for words! We were hurt and disappointed, as well as disgusted, that a Kentucky State Department was doing this to Kentuckians.

It happened that about a week later I had to go to Lexington to a hospital with one of our mothers. "Ha," I thought, "this is my chance." I had no idea who the President of the Kentucky Dental Association was, but knew I just had to get in touch with him, even if I had to go to Louisville. Fortunately, I found his office to be in Lexington. Calling him on the phone, I made an appointment, and the next day searched out his office. I expected to see a young "upstart," trying his wings, and wondered just how I would approach him. Much to my surprise, this president was a very gentle, kindly, elderly man, with beautiful, snow white hair! I was more disturbed than ever. But he soon made me feel quite at home. In our conversation, I mentioned Dr. Marks' coming, how he had written, and how the Dental Association had told him that because of a lack of reciprocity, he couldn't come.

"Yes, that's true," the president said.

"But we *have* to have him," I replied. "Our mountain folks have never had a chance to get to a dentist. The children need attention and care, and we're too far away to get it. Dr. Marks is a good friend who is coming to

153

help us, and we are ready for him. The folks will be so disappointed."

"I'm sorry," he replied, "but that's our state law, and he can't come into Kentucky from North Carolina to practice."

"But he's not coming to *practice*," I said. "He's just coming for a couple of days' clinic. He's making no charges. He's giving his time and skill—there is no other dentist near from whom he'll be taking patients. He's paying his own expenses, not expecting a penny in return."

"I'm very sorry," the president continued, "but I'll have to stick to the law; he cannot do dental work in Kentucky."

"Well," I said, "I'm sorry, too, and there's only one thing we can do about it."

"And what is that?" he asked.

"You come give the clinic."

He almost jumped from his chair, exclaiming, "Why, you know I can't do that!"

"Of course I know it," I replied. "If you or someone else from the Kentucky Dental Association had come, we would not have needed Dr. Marks. But our mountain folks have not had this help."

For a moment he was blank, but then, with a twinkle, said, "I'll tell you what. You write Dr. Marks to come, but don't tell me when he's coming. I won't know anything about it. It will be okay."

With eyes smiling, we shook hands, and I said a *big* thank you. Morris Fork was going to have its first dental clinic after all. There was to be considerable "reciprocity" between Morris Fork and Wilmington thereafter.

Sandy and his wife brought with them their maid, Magnolia. Before leaving Wilmington, they told Magnolia that the mountain folks might stare at her because many of them had never seen a Black woman.

"Well," she replied, "I ain't never seen a hillbilly either, so I reckon I'll do some staring too."

Sandy drove his Pontiac as far as Buckhorn, and we met his party with a jolt wagon and mules. The six miles

154

over a rough mountain trail, over huge boulders and through deep ruts was quite an experience. When they finally pulled up in front of the Community Center at Morris Fork, Magnolia looked around.

"I wonder who ever discovered this place!" she exclaimed.

Sam replied, "Why, Columbus did when he discovered all the rest of it."

Then, still rubbing her aching body, she sighed, "Well . . . they shore ain't done much to it since."

"At the beginning," Sandy Marks recalls, "the people were apprehensive and somewhat fearful. But when they learned that I used a surface anesthetic prior to injections which eliminated the pain of 'the needle' and that the injections eliminated the pain of extractions, they willingly and graciously accepted treatment.

"I did only emergency extractions and relieved pain. On each visit, I extracted about two hundred teeth for those living in Morris Fork.

"No problems were encountered with any of these extractions. However, one emergency did occur which did not prove to be serious. One small child had several abscessed primary teeth ('baby teeth') that constituted a health problem. In lieu of making several injections at one time which would be difficult, we decided that the best approach would be to put the child to sleep using ethyl chloride as the general anesthetic of choice. One adult watching the procedure through a window fainted cold and fell on the ground outside. He recovered quickly with no harmful effects."

As a result of coming face to face with great need and great opportunity in our midst at Morris Fork, Dr. Marks gave up his lucrative practice in Wilmington, sold his lovely home, and moved himself and his family to a needy spot in Africa. There, where likewise there had never been a dentist, he worked for years and started the very first dental school for native Africans in that part of the continent.

155

. . . Be kind
To one who cannot prove
He was a boy
By pointing to a tree, a house or creek
And saying from behind a rutted cheek,
"It was this world I was born into.
My father carried off this hill on his shoe
Into the house.
My mother swept it out."

Billy Edd Wheeler

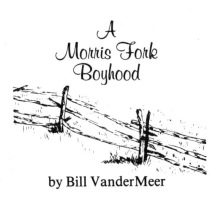

A Morris Fork Boyhood

by Bill VanderMeer

I'm indebted to my parents for many things, but I think one of the greatest debts that I owe them is a debt of gratitude for being brought up in a place like Morris Fork with the people that were there. It's a unique experience in this day and time. I've lived in less than fifty years what most people have not lived in eighty. I'm not old, but I've gone from horse and wagon into the jet age. It's an experience that I'm sorry all the kids in this country can't have; I'm sorry my children couldn't have lived it the way it was. I couldn't have been brought up with better folks than those of Morris Fork.

I remember lots of special things, things like getting up on a cold morning, going to the coalhouse to get a bucket of coal to get the fire started, having to carry kindling into the house every night, going to the barn and having Dad squirt warm milk into my mouth as he milked Old Bossy, going to Bud Thompson's store with a dime that would buy a gallon of kerosene and a "buuuunch" of good candy. Walking barefooted behind Rob Riley and his mule as he plowed the garden, looking for worms; after finding a good can of worms . . . slipping off with Briar Jim Riley to the creek for some fishing. Sitting on the river bank listening to Briar Jim tell his tales and not really caring whether you got a bite or not. Going to the one-room school carrying my lard pail lunch bucket with all the good things I'd eat, way before lunchtime. When we reached school, we all stood out in front and lined up, the biggest

157

kid up front on down the line to the littlest kid in back. Everybody stood at attention and saluted the flag and then we marched up the steps into the schoolhouse. Sitting there on a hot fall day, waiting for recess, finally the teacher would let us out and we'd run to get our game of "Round Town" going. "Round Town" was a game played with a broomstick, a rubber ball . . . and a bunch of happy kids. Sometimes we'd play "Mumbly Peg." If you lost, you could always look forward to a couple or three hours trying to get the grit out of your teeth. You got that when you had to get down and root the peg after Robert Thompson or one of the boys had really driven it into the ground with his knife.

These were the days when, if you misbehaved in school, you had to go out and cut your own switch, and if the size of the switch you brought back didn't suit the teacher, then you had to go out and get another one. After school, if it was still warm enough, we would head for the old swimming hole in the creek.

Sometimes I'd go up into the hills to find a perfect dogwood tree, to get the perfect stock for my new slingshot. A slingshot always had to have red rubbers; you had to get an inner tube that had red rubber in it. The black rubbers just weren't any good. Once in a while I'd get caught by Mom shooting at the birds in the yard, and have some privilege like going down and spending the night with Grannis Turner taken away from me. There was other fun . . . making popguns from the elm tree, where you'd cut the branch from a tree and take a stick and push what we'd call the pith out and then take another stick and carve it so it would fit down in the hole real tight with a knob on the end. Then you'd chew up one piece of paper and stuff it down in the end, then another—real wet— would go on top. Then you'd hit the stick with your hand and the pressure would kick the spit wad out of the bottom and the gun would make a real good pop so that somebody would holler!

Robert Thompson's father Bud had a truck that he used to haul groceries for his store. Every time he'd change a tire, Robert would bring the tire to school and we'd spend the day, one of us inside the tire being rolled over and over, while the other one was pushing, and if we got somebody we sort of didn't like, he always ended up in the creek.

Every fall we'd go up in the hills to one special place where we had a couple of hazelnut trees. We'd get the hazelnuts and skin 'em all out and bring them all back to school. We'd play "Hull Gull" with them. Either that or we'd go see Grannis who had a big hickory tree on his place. We'd go down and climb the tree, knock down the hickory nuts and play "Hull Gull" with those too. "Hull Gull" is a game where you put X amount of nuts in your hand, shake them up and you say to a guy "Hull Gull," and he says "six." If your nuts and his nuts add up to six, then he wins all your nuts.

First big event of the school year was the annual fair, which came around each September. The kids liked the games and the parties and everything, but they sure did hate to have to sit and listen to all those speeches which the 'old' people just kept going on and on with. The second big event of the year was the annual box supper. After you got to be in the third or fourth grade, then you started thinking about getting enough money together to buy a box from your special girl. Of course nobody could have a girl and no boys could like girls, but you still sorta thought about getting together 50 or 75 cents to buy a box. The schoolteacher would bring the girl up with her box which she'd have wrapped up in paper with ribbons on it, looking real pretty, and then you would bid on the box. And it always worked out that if somebody knew you wanted somebody's box, three or four people would get together and they'd bid you up. Generally everybody knew how much money you had, so if you had 75 cents, they'd get you up to 80 cents and you'd have to borrow another nickel or dime or you couldn't buy the box from the girl. Buying the box entitled you to eat with the girl, and after the social that night you got to walk her home. It was always part of the deal that you walked her home with a

That's me . . . behind Dad and Mary Elizabeth, with Mother holding "Silver's" bridle.

flashlight and you had to help her over a mudhole—sometimes you got to hold onto her hand for five or ten minutes after that. Later on in life you discovered they had in Morris Fork what was called "courtin' across the bed." If you were doing some serious courtin' with a girl, you'd take her home after a social or something and if the house only had two rooms in it, her people would all get to one side and give you and the girl the other room. Generally the only furniture in the room was a bed, a dresser and maybe one chair, so you'd sit and court across the bed.

Summers were a fine time. I always slept on the 'sleeping porch' and because it always got a little cool at night, I slept under about two tons of blankets. I had my dog "Burpee" who slept with me in a big old room that was screened in. Of course in winter, I couldn't sleep out there; it was too cold. But in the summer it was just fine.

The best things of the summer were fishing, hunting,

playing baseball, going to candy parties, and riding the horse across the hill to trade comic books with somebody over on Lucky Fork.

The worst parts of the summer were working in the garden, cleaning up around the yard, cutting grass, trying to get my sister to do some work ('cause she was pretty lazy). After Grannis moved down on the river, I used to ride the horse down and try to get him to go swimming, but his Dad would always make us work in the fields for about eight hours before he'd let us out that afternoon to go swimming.

During the war years, when I got home, right over the pulpit there was a stained glass window. I'd sit in there on Sunday morning and Dad would be preaching or they'd have some visiting preacher. Well, in this window there was a pane broken out, and it was broken in such a manner that it looked like a sailor. I could see his face and his hat and if I looked real close, I could see that he was holding a gun. This sailor and I fought the wars all the way from England to Germany, all the way from Pearl Harbor to Tokyo, and I don't really think that the U. S. would have won without our help every Sunday.

A lot of times after church, we'd go home with some of the people in the community for Sunday dinner. It's amazing, but up until I was about 14 years old I didn't know that a chicken had any parts except the head and feet. The kids always had to wait til the 'old' folks had finished eating, and the only things left were a few mashed potatoes and a little gravy, some cornbread, and the heads and feet from the chickens!

We kids always took part in just about all phases of mountain life . . . I'd go home with Robert Thompson and stay all night. If it was in the wintertime, just before we'd go to bed they'd get out a big basin of water and we'd all wash our feet. It would start with Robert's father and mother; then the oldest kids. Because I was the guest, I always got to go before Robert, but we all washed out of that same pan of water. By the time it got to us, it was cold and more than a little black. I really didn't see how it did any good, but we had to do it before we could go to bed.

Back when I was pretty young, I'd go up to stay all night with Robert quite a lot. That was when Uncle Lewis and Uncle Bud were both still living. We'd sit down in front of the fireplace, in the wintertime, and they'd bring out some apples and oranges. We'd peel the apples and eat the oranges. This was a big treat, because of the oranges and because they'd start telling these big tales.

One of their favorite tales was about a "painter," which is "mountainese" for about the same thing as a mountain lion. They'd talk about this one "painter" that really loved to get hold of little boys. And Uncle Lewis would give a squall like a "painter." Uncle Bud would say that he was talking to somebody the other day said they'd seen one just up at the head of the holler. Uncle Bud ran a store just across the creek. He had guns, fishing lines, just about everything a little boy would want . . . even tricycles. After he and Uncle Lewis would tell us the story of the "painter," he'd say, "Now we know you boys are pretty brave and if you'll go up to the toilet (which was about 100 yards up the creek) and slam the door so's we can hear it, then we'll let you go in and pick anything you want out of the store." So Robert and I would start out with each other. I'd dare him, and he'd double-dare me. We'd both go outside, get to the edge of the porch and start up towards the toilet. Then somebody'd make a sound, and we'd hightail it back in the house! We never did get up to that toilet, and consequently we never got to pick whatever we wanted from the store. But it's something I sure do remember.

Mother and Dad were the only Republicans on the creek; everybody else was a Democrat. I can remember going up to the store . . . Uncle Bud and Uncle Lewis would be sittin' in there with two or three men around the stove. Uncle Bud would say, "Bill, what are you? You a Republican or a Democrat?" If I'd say I was a Republican, they'd really get on me, but if I said I was a Democrat Uncle Bud would give me a piece of candy. And if I said I

162

was a Bud Thompson Democrat, I could have about anything I wanted in the store!

After I got up a little bigger, Dad would go out on a speaking trip somewhere and I'd have to ride over to Buckhorn on the horse to pick him up when he got off the train. I used to really enjoy those rides . . . except in the wintertime, when it got cold and dark real early. Sometimes, I'd have to ride part of the way in the dark. If Dad missed connections and didn't get in, then I'd have to ride all the way back across the mountain by myself. It wasn't too bad except for one place called Sweet Gum Ford. Sweet Gum Ford was the place where one of the biggest feuds in the state of Kentucky started: the Callahan/Dea-

A couple of Morris Fork boys stopping to talk with Dad in the middle of the creek—the only road we had!

ton Feud. All the people said Sweet Gum Ford was haunted.

The feud started over a canthook which was a piece of equipment that was used to move logs. I've forgotten whether it was a Callahan or a Deaton who was killed first, because somebody accused him of stealing a canthook. But folks used to say that if you caught it just right at night a Deaton or a Callahan would be crossing Sweet Gum Ford looking up and down for his canthook.

I used to have an old horse named Lucy. At one time she'd been a racehorse, but she broke down. But even after Dad got her, she could go pretty fast. I remember one time I went to Buckhorn to meet Dad and, sure enough, for some reason, he didn't come in. So I had to come back! Everything was pretty good, but when I got within a hundred yards of Sweet Gum Ford, I pulled Lucy up. I talked to her for a few minutes and told her we had to get across there pretty quick so if there was anybody looking for that canthook they wouldn't get hold of us. So I hit old Lucy a couple of times with a switch and we took off! Well, just on the other side of the creek, Lucy stumbled, and I went off! There I was, right in the middle of Sweet Gum Ford, and I knew for sure a Callahan or a Deaton was gonna get me cause I'd have to walk all the rest of the way home. I looked up and there was old Lucy down the road about twenty yards. She was stopped and she had her head turned around. She was just waiting for me. I really loved that old horse that night!

* * *

Reaching and Being Reached

The need for roads was, as it had been before at Wooton, a great need. Sam addressed it vigorously, in behalf of our entire Morris Fork area, especially after his return from North Carolina. This time, in the world outside, had re-sharpened his awareness of just how "cut off" and "left behind" we were in eastern Kentucky.

To reach Jackson, less than thirty miles away, we would ride horseback four miles to Buckhorn. This would take about two hours. At Buckhorn, we would try to get a truck to take us to Chavies—a fifteen mile trip. We could make this safely if it weren't too icy or snowy or if there weren't a "tide" from heavy rain to flood the road. Once into Chavies, we would finally board the train for the remaining twenty miles to Jackson. All this adventure to get to our county seat!

Henry Cravens recalled the time Edwin Morris was driving his Model T Ford down the creek towards Morris Fork. A big rain had been filling it rapidly. "Ed had to get out of his car and chain it to a tree. But the water got so high the cushions washed down the creek."

In and around Morris Fork, we had a good many road "workins." For these, both men and women would take shovels, hoes, any and all helpful tools, and with these—or their bare hands—move rocks and dirt to fill chug holes and level bumpy stretches. In spite of their efforts, a team of mules would often have to come to the rescue of a vehicle trying to make its way over the last miles to us.

In one of the taped interviews Sam completed before he died, he recalled our battle for roads.

. . . we went to the State Department with delegations. They would say, 'Well, why did you build those churches and schools in those out-of-the-way places and then expect the state to build roads to them?' I would count to ten, and then I would say, 'They happen to be Kentuckians.'

"I said, 'What if you were a minister and you were asked to preach the funeral of a person whose life you know could have been saved if there had been good roads to travel?'

"One of our little boys stepped on a rusty needle while we were having a mattress making project. We tried as quickly as we could to get him to Lexington so he could have a shot for lockjaw. It meant taking that little fellow on a stretcher over swollen creeks into

Owsley County, and then taking him on horseback to Booneville where we could get a car. Then from Booneville we would drive him to Lexington . . .

I saw the father and mother come back with that child's body in a casket on a pole . . . just a little bundle on a pole, and they wanted me to say it was God's will, when I knew it was the Highway Department's fault. If we had had a road, this child could have been gotten out in a couple of hours; his life would have been spared. I had to dress that child in my own child's clothing, make a coffin and see to his heartbroken parents.

Another of our boys slid down a hill and punctured his rectum on a piece of root. We needed to get him out to the railroad. We went back to see if he were comfortable, and he was dead—in the homemade sled drawn by mules we had used, trying to get him to a hospital."

Like Miss McCord, Sam never gave up. He never accepted the insensitive notion that because our mountain folks didn't have money or cars they somehow didn't need and deserve good roads.

After we had managed to get our State Highway Commissioner to accept an invitation to journey over to see us, his staff people in Frankfort looked at their maps for Booneville and Morris Fork, and said confidently, "We can make that in two hours." Well, they were due at our house at six o'clock for dinner, and they arrived at ten o'clock! The men who drove the jeep were state policemen who had driven in the war. They said they had never encountered anything overseas like what they did trying to get to Morris Fork. The Commissioner quickly joined the campaign for our roads.

Soon after, we got a stretch of road from Booneville to Morris Fork. But we still needed a piece from Cow Creek. It was eventually built, but it was the beginning of the Sixties before this gravel road became a paved one. How exciting it was when someone exclaimed, "The blacktop's just five miles away!"

After some crooked places were made straight and some rough places plain, a wonderful musical and spiritual exchange became possible for us. The eighty miles of arduous travel that had before seemed to keep Berea and Morris Fork almost impossibly apart now helped to join them.

Soon after World War II, our dear Berea College faculty friend, Emma Reeverts, brought her colleague Rolf Hovey and his wife to visit us. From this new friendship came Rolf's interest in bringing many of his Berea choral students to present "The Messiah" and other beautiful music for us for several years. On one occasion, a separate group of Centre College students made their own long journey from Danville to sing by the light of our candles and kerosene lamps.

But the most exciting journey was the one we made many times, with our young folks especially, to hear the glorious, full scale performance of "The Messiah" in Berea.

Such planning and scheming for this, one more unheard-of event for Morris Fork. We had to make plans to secure a bus, to have the children excused from school. We had to see about proper clothing, prepare a lunch, collect all the children and start the long eighty mile trip shortly after noon. We will never forget the thrill of arriving in glistening, decorated Berea—then the beautiful Union Church—so breathlessly shining with Christmas. The crowd was overflowing. We had to stand for the two-hour program. But the great orchestra—the choirs filling the entire platform—the people! The most wonderful music we had ever heard poured forth, the story of Christmas became more real, and our very souls were lifted. Not even the long journey home, over dark and slippery mountain roads, and our arrival at 3:00 a.m. could take away the glow of this wonderful night.

When it was ended, one of our mothers who had made the journey said, "I ain't never seed nothin' like this—I ain't never heerd nothin' like this. I'm comin' back next year!" And come back we did, many times over.

The Community House . . . hostel and home to a heap o' livin'.

168

8
The Abundant Fifties

Charles and Emily Egbert became members of our Morris Fork family in 1951. What a blessing they were!

Emily was a registered nurse, Charles a Bible school graduate *and* an electrician. The mountain community to which they had gone initially did not put their eagerness and talents to use, so they had pretty much decided to go home to Philadelphia and their regular work there.

"If the Lord won't use us here . . . " Charles said to Sam.

Before Charles could reach a pessimistic conclusion to that thought, Sam responded. "Charles, the Lord moves in a mysterious way his wonders to perform. He has sent us an electrician and a good man just when we needed one. We need both you and Emily at Morris Fork to help us. Won't you stay?"

Charles worked day and night to wire our Community House and many of our Morris Fork homes. When he called on me in Berea one afternoon, he recalled how—on the first Sunday we had our own electricity—Sam had built his sermon around the event, pointing out that the electric light (like spiritual light) exposed "cobwebs" in the corners that had never been seen before.

Before our electricity was connected, I had asked Sam if he didn't think that perhaps we ought to have a Delco generator in the Community House which could serve the

Some years ago a mountaineer was at the local store when a salesman rode up on a mule with his sample cases. When he came into the store and showed some of his samples, the old man looked eagerly at the new and "quer" things the stranger had brought. The salesman saw his interest and offered him a banana. The old man looked at it curiously and then, very firmly, refused to sample it. When the salesman insisted, the old man said, "I ain't never et none of them things an I got along just fine. If I was to eat it I might like hit and crave more. I kain't get all the things I'm cravin' now so I better not start a new cravin'."

Well, we fear that we have started a lot of "cravin's" in Morris Fork . . . windows, rugs, pictures on the wall, wallpaper, fresh fruit, good clothing, education, pianos, variety in garden and field, roads, electricity, better stock,—all these and many more.

—Sam VanderMeer

church also. "Well," he replied, "you know, there is no money for it, and I don't think we ought to get too far ahead of our folks. I don't want them to think I'm above my raisin' . . . kerosene lamps will do for a while yet." Sam seemed to appreciate the fact that a missionary had better not get too blessed with conveniences . . . too comfortable!

Sam had also found it necessary to strike a blow against the misuse of progress. As Charles remembers it, Sam became rather irate when he learned that our local store proprietor had taken to selling cold beer from his soft drink cooler. Sam confronted him, saying that it was only because of the church in the first place that electricity had come as far as Morris Fork and had been connected to several places. The proprietor stopped selling beer.

Emily was a great help, using her nursing skills in midwifery whenever they were needed. Her talent with the violin also provided some lovely additions to our worship services.

A happy reunion with Charles and Emily reminded me of how we had brought to all the instances of serious illness that confronted us every resource of prayer and skill we could muster or reach. We recalled the time in the Fifties when one of our families refused medical care for their little girl who was suffering with spinal meningitis. Emily finally persuaded the father that prayer alone was not enough in this case. With her strong urging, he wrapped the youngster in blankets and "packed" her three miles over the hills to an awaiting automobile that carried her to the hospital in Lexington. She survived—and about a month later, her father presented Charles and Emily with thirteen chickens.

As time passed, and it did so quickly with so much happening during those years, there came a day when Charles called Sam aside.

"I've made this a matter of much deep prayer, Sam, in response to the way the Lord has led me and what He's done for us here. I want to go into the ministry. I want to be His preacher. But I don't have the education for this."

With continued prayer, the way opened for Charles to go to Berea College for a couple of years and then on to Georgetown College to complete his undergraduate degree studies. From Georgetown he entered the Presbyterian Seminary in Louisville, where he completed his ministerial preparation.

This Philadelphia electrician, who had helped to bring light to Morris Fork, Kentucky, was now prepared to bring it—in other ways—to other corners of creation.

At the time of our retirement from Morris Fork, we received a short but very touching letter from Charles and Emily. In it were these words . . .

"When a young couple came riding over the hill one July morning to greet Uncle Sam and Aunt Nola, little did they realize that that day was a high point in their lives. For they not only met the people of Morris Fork, but found a father and mother."

This letter was a high point in *our* lives.

In our Christmas letter for 1951, we couldn't help highlight such exciting progress as the coming of electricity and the reaching out of the state highway system towards us. But it was something very traditional that provided the opening note of the letter:

Early on Christmas morning we were talking in the kitchen, just Sam and I . . . early because we felt we must have a "head start" for the busy day ahead. And even tho it was chock full, there seemed one more necessary item—a cake to be baked for the two young VanderMeers home from school! Since the previous days had been far too full to allow this "necessary luxury," we had decided to sneak it in before the grand rush of the day had begun. We were in the midst of the preparation, also trying to make a few more definite plans for the coming activities, when it happened—the call to come, quickly, for a confinement case! Sam said, "Well, it wouldn't be Christmas without a baby." It had happened so many times in the years gone by—a brand new baby right in the middle of all the grand Christmas rush of the many activities.

Of course a new Christmas baby is much more important than a Christmas cake, so hurriedly pushing aside these preparations, the nurse's bag was brought out for inspection and checked for necessary items. A double layette, some of the very baby things you all sent for Christmas, was packed. Clothing was changed to a riding outfit, with nurse's uniform and apron tucked in saddle pockets. We were soon loaded atop old Silver and off up the muddy creek road to the little cabin some two miles away—in the rain.

The usual hectic pre-Christmas rush had been going on for a month, when hours, even days and nights, had been spent opening, sorting, tagging, the many wonderful gifts you had sent for this Morris Fork Christmas. Did you ever try getting Christmas ready for some 500 folks—right within your very own four walls? [We did not even mention all the letter thank-yous that had to be written.—N. V.]

Christmas afternoon, in spite of a hard rain just at the time for service, the little church was well filled for the "family Christmas." This is the time when candles on the tree are lighted, the testimonies are given, reminding us of our Lord's goodness. And, wonder of wonders, this year, for the first time in history, with the lighted candles, electric light bulbs also glowed in the tree! We were celebrating our very first Christmas with electricity! The glow of the lights, the deep, rich beauty of the little sanctuary, the beautiful native decorations of spruce, pine and holly, the happy excitement of the children, babies' voices, radiant faces of mothers and fathers—all made a picture not soon forgotten. And as the smaller children presented a living picture of the Nativity scene, under Miss Berger's direction, we felt this a most precious Christmas at Morris Fork.

One entire evening was given to our group of high school people home for the holidays. They came, eighteen of 'em, to our house for a chili supper. And we were proud and happy to have them, home from high school and college. Only when one knows something of the struggle and very great effort all down through these 25 years, will he understand and appreciate the thrill of this group! We included 2 servicemen home on furloughs. But sixteen Morris Forkers away in school! It does not seem possible Morris Fork could have achieved that—when but a few short years ago, nobody went to school, nor did anybody want to go to school! No wonder we count this a highlight.

Along with our electricity we are celebrating our first Christmas to be on the highway. Yes sir, within a mile of our community house, is a state highway! Now, for the first time in our history, we'll have a dry land road, instead of our present one—made of water!

*   *   *

When I told Cathy Berger, our fine "brought on" teacher from New Jersey, that I was going to try to pick up the Morris Fork story from where Sam, on God's calling, had put it down, she said she wanted to recall what she could of her years (1949-1953) with us. Knowing how spiritedly she had lived out those years for all of her pupils and as a member of our household, I wasn't surprised that she sent along a memory quilt of her own. Cathy's little red Model A Ford is fixed in my memory as quite a patch of moving color itself. Cathy wrote:

I sure remember Aunt Sallie Riley. At 80, she would outlast all of us in the Friday night skipping games! And we'd have seventy-five or more of our young people for those. Even the most shy got drawn in by Sam . . .

It was always a delicate matter to carry the lamps,

filled with kerosene, from the Community House over to the school for our games . . .

One time—on the way to Lucky Fork—Elmer Cornett actually let me hold on to the tail of his horse in order to get pulled up the mountainside . . .

Another time, when my folks came down from New Jersey for a visit, they got stranded on the way in. Some folks took them in for a chicken dinner and then gave them a midnight wagon ride into Morris Fork. My mother had to really hold on tight when the wagon tipped, as it occasionally did, on two wheels! . . .

It was pretty exciting when my eighth graders of 1953 took two of the three top places in the county exams . . . (One of my older seventh graders said once, "H'ain't never heerd tell uv a teacher make us work all day!") . . .

I had fifty-one youngsters in Grades 1 to 8. I'd teach Grades 1 to 4 from 8:00 a.m. to noon and Grades 5 to 8 from 12:30 p.m. to 4:30 p.m. On cold days, everyone took turns sitting close to the potbellied stove. Those who were wettest from getting to school, and the youngest, had first choice. One of the older boys would make the fire, but I had to be my own janitor. Occasionally someone would put some buckshot in the coal skuttle!

There was an outhouse around back of the school and, out front, a well that I arranged to get covered. Before this, it used to really scare me to look out and see two boys up on the stone wall of it, drawing up the bucket.

I remember when someone wanted to name a new son after Sam, and Sam smilingly said he wasn't going to have any namesake of his living in a house without a window . . . so he paid to have one built!

Sam would find a new way to say "Catherine" every time he called me in the morning.

I remember the time we unpacked a wagonload of Christmas packages that had come in from outside and found a cake of soap marked, "For Boy, Age 10." We

175

couldn't quite figure out why a cake of soap should have been so carefully earmarked!

But one of the cutest moments was the time we were riding on the truck and crossing the river going away from Morris Fork. Naomi Riley looked back and yelled . . . "Goodbye, good ole U.S.A.!"

In mid January of 1952, Cathy provided our youngsters with one of their greatest adventures. On a very cold morning, and after a fifteen-mile combined horseback and truck journey, she—and her brood of forty-six pupils—boarded L. and N. Train No. 4 at Chavies for a twenty-five mile rail trip to Jackson, our closest "big city." Cathy had arranged in advance for everyone to have some special sightseeing hours at *The Jackson Times,* the post office and in several stores.

The story of this railroading adventure was featured in the L. and N. Magazine of March, 1952. The author of the article described some of the excitement of the youngsters, most of whom—even then, in 1952—had never even seen a train:

"New thrills came every minute . . . The very luxury of sitting by a big coach window as the landscape sped by . . . of gulping from a paper cup of water drawn by a little tap . . . of nibbling at box lunches meant for noontime, while Conductor Sam Rainey punched the tickets and asked if all was well . . . of knowing the mysterious wonder of speeding through dark tunnels as the locomotive whistle sounded sonorously."

The spirit that Cathy Berger "brought on" and instilled in our youngsters was a lasting gift. It provided inspiration as well as happy memories.

*   *   *

And how well I remember a certain 17-year-old boy from Harrisburg, Pennsylvania! When I asked Bob

176

Undercuffler, now on the pastoral staff of the North-minister United Presbyterian Church in Cincinnati, to recall some of his memories of camp and later days at Morris Fork, he had much to tell:

During our second week of Vacation Bible School, our group from Harrisburg decided that we wanted to do something of lasting value for the people of Morris Fork. We decided that we would erect a cross on the hillside overlooking the community. I believe there had been a cross placed there some years earlier, but it had fallen down. That was a whole lot of work. Some of the boys from our junior high class helped with the project. As a matter of fact, they did most of the chopping. Larry McMaster considered himself to be quite an axeman, but he quickly turned the job over to "Uncle Sol" Riley and some other young fellows. We then

Cathy Berger's Morris Fork students ready to reboard the train at Jackson for their return trip. Calvin Morris, at left, helped out as trip escort. (PHOTO BY JACK KUPRION)

carried buckets of whitewash up that steep hill and whitewashed the cross.

On the final Sunday that we were at Morris Fork, following the service of worship, the congregation left the church and went out on the road where they could look up at the hillside. Sam said some words about the cross and the significance of it in the life of Christian people, and then waved a white handkerchief to those of us up on the hillside. We started the difficult task of hoisting the cross into the deep hole we had dug. As we erected it, the congregation below us sang, "When I Survey the Wondrous Cross." When we got the cross into place, we stood back and looked . . . and listened . . . and sang too . . .

> Were the whole realm of nature mine,
> That were a present far too small.
> Love so amazing, so divine,
> Demands my soul, my life, my all.

Hearts and eyes were overflowing with tears of great thanksgiving—all singing seemed to stop as we came to that last line.

I remember one Friday night we were playing "Skipping Games" in the Morris Fork School. There was a very large crowd of people there . . . we sang, skipped, and clapped for several hours—almost non-stop. Sam led it all. I remember, however, that during a brief break someone came in and said to Sam that there was some trouble out in the school yard. I was next to Sam at the time, so I followed him to see what was happening. Two big, burly young men had evidently had too much to drink, and they were talking loud and trying to stir up a fight. Sam put his arms around the young men, called them by name and said, "We don't want to have any trouble here tonight, do we?" They replied, "No, Uncle Sam, we don't, we're just goin' home." They then walked off the school grounds. Sam walked right back into the school, began clapping his

178

hands, getting people back into the circle, and off we went with more skipping games.

During the summer of 1954, a woman by the name of Mary Morris, who lived up at the head of Morris Fork Creek, was ill and bedfast. So Uncle Sam suggested one afternoon that we go up and meet her, sing to her, and pray with her . . . I remember we crossed back and forth through the creek, and several times had to walk in the creek because the hillsides were so steep. Sam reminded us that for years Mary Morris had walked faithfully this way to church and then home again. She also attended women's meetings and other functions of the church.

Mary was in bed when we got there . . . She had a hymn book, and she suggested that we sing several hymns from it. Some of them were new to us, but we tried our best. When she shared with us her trust in God and in His love for her life, it was a simple testimony, and it made a tremendous impression on me . . . ·

The scene Bob recalls here is still vivid in my own memory. I can see Mary—and hear her talkin' to those young "brought on" folks from Pennsylvania. It didn't matter; she talked as if she had known them all her life.

Mary knew it wasn't going to be too long until she would enter that beautiful eternal home—with no more sickness, no more pain. In spite of the pain now, her sweet face was smiling. She spoke quietly but earnestly of what God and the church had meant: "You all be good and do what God wants you to do. He'll be good to you, just like he's been good to me."

So deep was the impression Mary Morris' faith had upon Bob Undercuffler that soon after this he made the decision to commit his own life to Christ.

Throughout his years as a student at Grove City College in Pennsylvania and, later, at Princeton Theological Seminary, he stayed closely in touch with all of us at Morris Fork through our work camps and in other ways.

Sam was dedicating a good portion of his time in the early Sixties to the revitalization of the church over at Buckhorn, where a new dam and man-made lake had just been completed. He reached out to Bob, who was in his final year of seminary studies. Bob reached back and by the summer of 1962 was at Buckhorn as minister there. He and his bride Pat were very special neighbors to us. When their infant son died of pneumonia in the late autumn, they drew even closer to us. It was one of our saddest hours but one in which Sam reminded all of us, "The Eternal God is your dwelling place, and underneath are everlasting arms."

*　　*　　*

Rather late one Saturday afternoon, after our new dirt road in from the highway had been built along the creek, a car drove up to the community house. A lady, entirely unknown to us, got out and came up to the door. "I'd like to stay here tonight and for the weekend," she said.

"Alright," I replied, though I was a bit puzzled. "We have no other visitors now and our guest room happens to be empty." While getting in her baggage and becoming settled, she talked very pleasantly. During our evening meal, she asked if there were Sunday services, saying she'd like to attend. After we told her of our Sunday schedule, she said she'd probably be with us until after Sunday dinner.

While getting ready for bed, I said to Sam that I thought there seemed something very strange about this woman's coming. Still she seemed quite pleasant to have about.

After the Sunday morning service, when she came back to the house, she appeared a bit dejected and bewildered. "I don't know how to say this—I don't know what to do," she said. Then she went on to explain how folks at church had told her about the community center and who we were. "I thought this was a motel in a little mountain town," she said. "I had no idea it was your home, or that this is a mission station. I don't know what to do about it, except to ask you to forgive my ignorance. But," she went on, "there is one thing else I do want to say. I live in Lexington, in a big house, all by myself. Anytime you come over, I want you to call me. If you ever dare to go to a hotel or motel—well, I just won't forgive you. I want you to promise me that you will make my house your headquarters anytime you come to Lexington."

And we did just that! The time Billy Graham had the Lexington Crusade, we lived with Eleanor Carey for a week. She was most gracious and kind, and she has been a wonderful friend ever since.

Cast your bread upon the waters...

Many times, with groups coming to visit from other churches, the question would be asked, "What can we do? What do you need now?" With such earnest desire to help, many were welcomed to tasks of painting, redoing old furniture, working in the yard and garden, doing odd jobs at the church, assisting in cases of illness or any emergency.

While visiting our very helpful Southport Church in Indianapolis, talking to a women's group, this question was freshly asked. Thinking quickly, though hesitant to ask for so much, I said, "Do you really want to know one of our biggest needs right now?" Reassured that they did, indeed, but still a bit hesitant, I said, "Well, our creek bed roads have been improved. We have a gravel road up on the hill out of the creek now, and we do need a car of some description—preferably a station wagon—to meet our community needs."

A slight gasp and a look of mild surprise ran through the crowd. This was a bit different from asking for "old clothing!" But the leader managed a smile, saying, "We'll take this up with our session, and if at all possible, we'll be happy to at least help to get this station wagon." "Oh, thank you," I almost breathlessly replied, with something of a blush.

And one sunny day, not too many weeks later, here

Our new 1950 Ford, from the folks of Southport Church in Indianapolis, fords its way toward us.

Welcome to Morris Fork. The new road, a cut above the old one . . . the creek below.

182

came some of our Southport church folks, wending their way very carefully over our new narrow, rough gravel road, in a brand new Ford station wagon! It was, somehow, a gift and tribute to our trusty Fred and "Hi-O" Silver, who through these early years had carried us so faithfully and safely. They had borne us, and many other people, from here and there, so many miles through mud—rain—snow—ice—over the mountain trails—through the creeks. Now, their treks could be less burdened.

In the very midst of the abundant Fifties, Sam sat down to prepare our Christmas letter . . .

It doesn't seem possible that a whole year [1955] has passed since I sat at this same desk, by the same window and looked upon a scene practically the same as the one I see as I write this Christmas letter. Once more the hills are covered with snow, the branches of the trees forming a black tracery against the heavy grey sky, and the little brown church still nestles so peacefully in its setting of hemlock, rhododendron and mountain laurel. Out on the lawn a group of school boys are having an hilarious time snowballing. A woman has just come into the house from over on the other side of the mountain to ask "Miss Nola" to come and give "Uncle Berry" a shot of medicine the doctor left for him. He is "bad off" and of course "Miss Nola" will go and give him the medicine. Young "H. S." Stamper has just come across the church lawn with a team of mules and a wagon load of coal which was mined out of the mountainside almost two miles down the creek. And so life goes on with the every day duties calling for attention and the scraps of gay wrapping paper and tinsel reminding us that Christmas has come and gone. Did I say gone? Gone as a date perhaps but such an experience as Christmas at Morris Fork is really never gone. It becomes part of you and goes on with you, lending its glory to each new day.

Ever since Christmas, when groups gather together,

they start talking about the various experiences we had during the holidays. Some declare the parties were best, others the motion pictures, others the happy experience of singing carols; but the groups of High School students who went on the hike through the Buffalo country know that their experience was best of all! So, let me tell you about it.

On the Friday after Christmas, about twenty teenagers started with us for this all day hike. It was very cold and there was some wind and snow. We had great fun climbing the mountain trail that led us from Breathitt County, over the Loudema Gap, into Owsley County and into the almost virgin forest of Buffalo. In a small clearing where Zack Yeary and his family live in a log cabin, we stopped to cook our dinner. We found that wet, green wood doesn't burn very readily even though each boy named the fire for his truelove! But we finally cooked our meal, played "Whoop-Hide" and "Base" and started down Buffalo Creek to the Lucky Fork Church House. At one time this was an out station of Morris Fork, but we turned it over to the Rev. Mr. and Mrs. Chester Ranck and their staff. After a brief rest there and the singing of carols in the lovely rustic church, we said goodbye to Selma Johnson, the Lucky Fork nurse, and traveled to the head of Will Baker's Branch. Here we sang more carols and started over the mountain back into Breathitt County. Such a time as we had coming down this steep mountainside—such sliding—such laughing—such screaming! At the foot of the mountain we stopped to sing carols at the home of Jeff and Mary Morris—and then we went inside to have a short service by Mary's bedside. She loved having the young folks come to share their gaiety, their songs and their prayers. As we came down the creek at the edge of dark, practically all the young had found a partner and hand in hand they came, singing as they walked along. It had been a full, happy day and now physically tired, all hearts were

Santa Claus—one of our high school students, Lonnie Turner—makes his rounds, clanging a school bell along the way. This Associated Press photo appeared all across the country on Christmas Day, 1967.

185

By firelight, Danny Caudill puffs out shaky notes on his new trumpet. Santa (Leon Morris) had to remove his mask to show Danny how it's done. (PHOTO BY KARL G. KARSCH)

"Uncle Sam" gets some enthusiastic help sorting Christmas parcels that have just arrived at our Morris Fork post office. (PHOTO BY CARL G. KARSCH)

... Comes to Morris Fork

Sam directing the decoration of the sanctuary. All the fresh greens have just been cut from our hills. (PHOTO BY CARL G. KARSCH)

The church—and Morris Fork School— dressed in snow.

Zack Yeary and his mule rest a minute after bringing in our Christmas holly from Buffalo Creek—1958. (PHOTO BY CARL G. KARSCH)

glad that they lived in a place where folks had learned to do such nice things together . . .

And now the day has come to a close. The boys who threw snowballs on the lawn are asleep. "Uncle Berry" has had his medicine and the neighbors will watch over him during the night. Some of the coal that "H. C." brought is burning in the open fireplace. Outside, the big living Christmas tree glows once more, shedding a glory on the new fallen snow. And out in the big world there are all of you who have prayed and shared and sacrificed to help make possible this place where the love of God is shed abroad through Jesus Christ our Lord.

Floods had been all too familiar happenings ever since Wooton days. But, somehow, with so much positive change happening around us over the years, we weren't really psychologically ready for the way the waters came upon us two years later. As they began to subside, we managed to peck out a letter to the friends we knew would be worrying about us.

January 31, 1957

Dear Folks:

We are in the throes of a flood—the worst in Kentucky mountain history, according to "old settlers." Have had incessant rain, day and night, for almost a week. As our mountain creeks and streams gained momentum, reaching the size of raging torrents, overflowing their banks, we feared the worst; and it has come.

Here at Morris Fork we are high enough to be out of immediate danger, and are unharmed. But our little road, a mile away, was blocked, and back water came within a couple miles of us. Damage and suffering in surrounding communities are not entirely known, but we know there has been much loss and dire trouble. We have heard of no deaths, tho many families are homeless. Houses, literally, washed away. Where buildings have stood against the pounding water, the water has entered, washing away furniture—bedding—cloth-

189

ing; in fact, all worldly possessions of these folk, leaving a muck of mud and water, with walls, floors, what furniture remained, a soggy, deadly loss. In our little out-station, Crockettsville, many homes were so damaged families spent the night in the hills—in the cold, hard rain, as water drove them from their homes. The little schoolhouse, where we've had S.S. [Sunday School] all these years, was picked up, turned squarely around, floated to another corner of the yard! Parts of the building are still intact, but windows are smashed, floors ruined, walls soaked, looks as tho the last S.S. session has been held there! Sam went to Crockettsville today—what is left of it!—to find the score and see our next move to help. To those of you who know Beech and Elizabeth Turner, the water was within 9 feet of their house. John Owen's car, in the driveway, was completely covered!

Our adjoining community of Buckhorn has been all but wiped out. Stores, homes, filled with water—many of them being wiped away. Barns, with winter storage of hay, corn, coal piles—all gone. One woman lost 60 hens. Some animals drowned. Surrounding towns—Hazard, Corbin, Whitesburg, Jackson, Barbourville, Beattyville—suffered much. Reports are that loss at Hazard is something like $9,000,000.

No mail in or out yesterday; so far none today. Electricity off since Tuesday. We're holding our breath about freezer filled with food—partly school lunch—supposed to 'hold' 72 hours! If reports of damaged power plant are true, no telling when the current will be back. Poles—wires—are down on every hand, stretched the miles between here and Hazard. Looks as tho we're going back to the dark ages!

We are very thankful for God's care in this extremity. There has been no loss of life, no deadly fires. Still a cold drizzle today. We pray it shall cease, that He will send the warm sunshine to "dry us out"; that there shall be no serious complications of sickness. Will you pray with us that we shall be able to help, in this great time of need—that we shall be brought closer to Him, realizing anew His great power—our utter dependence upon Him.

We sincerely hope the worst is over. You'll be hearing again, but wanted this word to get to you. Know you'll pardon the carbons; it's the quickest way we could reach you all.

Lovingly,
"Saminola"

Such swift and substantial hardship was met, of course, as other hardship had been met before. Our folks helped one another in whatever ways they could, and our friends who were part of Morris Fork—although they were many miles away—sent us their concern and assistance. The abundance of such neighborly care, near and far, was one of our greatest riches.

Our young folks ready to step off in the annual Morris Fork Community Fair parade.

Sam's garden in midsummer. Campers stayed in cabin at left and converted barn at right.

9
Final Progress
1960-1969

When I've noted that letters and carbons were "the quickest way" to reach our friends, I was of course acknowledging that there were no telephones as yet to link us to the world that bustled with them out beyond us. Their ring was not heard until 1968. Then it was exciting to realize that at last our thoughts and messages could flow from Morris Fork to the Mississippi and beyond . . . as only the water of our little creek had done for so long.

In between the excitement of our first electricity and our first telephones, some of our folks, urged on and helped financially by those who had gone to take jobs beyond the mountains, began to put in that luxury of luxuries: the bathroom! I remember hearing about one of our mothers showing off and explaining the new facility to her little boy. In utter amazement, the little fellow said . . . "You mean we can go outdoors in the house?"

By the 1950s, our Morris Fork Community Fair had grown to become not merely the fulfillment of our harvest season, but one of our strongest and happiest traditions. (Our last fair in 1969 produced over 4,000 exhibits!)

With considerable help from county home agents, the quality of our produce and crafts improved so much that articles were selected for the State Fair in Louisville. Some of these earned first and second prizes there.

Each year, on the eve of the fair, we would have all of our judges—county officials, University extension specialists, garden club representatives, and other visitors from distant points—join us at the Community House for dinner and a happy social hour.

Then it was down to business . . . the judging of what seemed to be countless exhibits over at the schoolhouse. The large number of these in later years would keep the judges busy until 2:00 a.m. or later. Until electricity came in 1951, all our after dark judging was done by the light of kerosene lamps!

After a few winks, our big day would be upon us. A morning parade of children and teachers from many surrounding schools would end at the church, where a special service, offering thanks for the harvest and the fellowship of it would mark the "official" opening of the fair. How vividly I remember the very first appearance of a band at Morris Fork. Our folks were completely in awe of the instruments of the Breathitt County High School youngsters and the wonderful sounds that came forth from them.

In a taped chat with some Lees College students, Sam described our system for recognition and prizes:

"We gave prizes for the family booth. But we never gave cash prizes. What we would do is to have a score sheet and total the number of points that a family would get. The points would count for the ribbons: red, white, blue or purple ribbons—each one would have a certain number of points . . . We would total those points and then we would make up what was called the Family Package. We would save up the whole year for it. It would have towels, sheets, and pillow cases; things for a family—curtains and maybe a pretty picture. The number of points to the size of the package. So some didn't get perhaps but a little package. But that was a starter."

The listing below was taken from a section of our entry blanks for one of our fairs:

LOT F

Ring # 1 1 pair pillow cases
" 2 1 Luncheon Set
" 3 1 Kitchen Apron
" 4 1 Cotton Dress
" 5 1 piece of patching
" 6 3 Button Holes
" 7 1 made over garment
" 8 1 boy's shirt
Ring # 9 1 ladies gown
" 10 1 baby's dress
" 11 1 child's Bloomer Dress
" 12 1 sample of darning
" 13 1 piece of knitting
" 14 1 handmade scarf
" 15 Pillow top

LOT J   HOMEMADE KITCHEN PRODUCTS

Ring # 1 1 dish cottage cheese
" 2 1 dish homemade butter
" 3 1 bar homemade soap
" 4 1 loaf yeast Bread
" 5 1 loaf or cake Gingerbread
Ring # 6 1 pone corn bread
" 7 1 cake
" 8 6 biscuits
" 9 1 plate candy
" 10 6 muffins
" 11 1 pie
" 12 6 doughnuts

For a number of years, Nevyle Shackelford, correspondent for *The Lexington Leader,* kept a watch over the fair's growth and progress. In one of his columns, he not only paid a tribute to the hard work of all our folks, but summed up so nicely the character and spirit of what, in our hopes, we had set out to do.

MORRIS FORK, Ky.—The Morris Fork School and Community Fair which is held each year in this faraway corner of Breathitt County is an amazing event. In fact, it is doubtful if there is anything like it in the entire state. It not only represents community development in its highest form, but is an excellent ex-

195

ample of a more important form of development—human development . . .

. . . the community is made up of 119 families. They are widely scattered up and down the narrow valley of the creek and over the mountainous area. This year at the fair these families entered more than 3,000 exhibits, each one of such excellence that the ability of the judges who awarded the ribbons was sorely taxed . . .

One room in the Morris Fork School building contained so many sewing exhibits that it resembled a big city department store having a bare wall sale. Another room appeared as a florist shop, and no bakery ever featured a larger selection of cakes, cookies, pies, bread, candy, and other items originating in the kitchen than was displayed in one room of the nearby church. Actually all this has to be seen to be fully believed.

For a long time officials of country agricultural fairs have complained that every year they experience great difficulty in getting folks to bring in exhibits. They offer cash prizes and other forms of inducement, but still the exhibits are often scanty. Not so at Morris Fork. Encouraged by "Uncle Sam" VanderMeer, folks haul exhibits in by the sled load . . .

There are no Ferris wheels, carousels, or rides to attract. But there is, nevertheless, much fun to be had . . .

The Morris Fork Fair is a community event in which all participate in one way or another. Even babies are fetched sometimes and exhibited. Everybody seems to bring and show off something, like 88-year-old Jerry Morris, who brought along a homemade grubbing hoe, an ox yoke, and a fiddle. And like Aunt Lydia Helton, now in her late 90s, who set up a very attractive booth displaying her spinning wheel, the articles she made from the thread spun with it, and a fireplace over which hung an old-fashioned cast iron bean kettle.

Taking them as a whole, Morris Fork folks live somewhat "out of the way," but if their fair is any indication of their life and living conditions, which it surely must be, then it is extremely doubtful if people anywhere live better, have any more of the basic needs, or have a better time.

Very soon after settlin' in at Morris Fork, we had realized there were many outlying folks who needed help. So, "outstations" became a part of our program. Since these communities were all some three to five horseback miles from our center, we wondered how we could serve them all. Since we couldn't get seven Sunday services into one short Sabbath day, we decided to hold several Sunday School services on Saturday. Where there were schools in these communities, I visited them for immunizations and developed as much of a health program as was possible. I went to all these communities for "baby cases" when called and urged folks to come to Morris Fork as much as possible for any and all activities. We reached out, with Sunday School and other activities, to the little communities of Sandlin, Crockettsville, Freeman's Fork, Deaton Branch, Courtland, and Burton Fork—all situated on different branches of Long's Creek. All entailed horseback trips to isolated families—families who would not have been touched or helped had not the church heard the Macedonian cry and come to help.

Sebastian's Branch, our last "outstation," was developed in 1967. It is a well populated community about six miles from Morris Fork, on the road to Jackson. A large consolidated grade school had been opened by the county at Turner's Creek, about three miles from Sebastian's Branch, and by this time a black top highway had been constructed. There were more families living along the highway, and nothing had been done for them in the way of community activities. When we started Sunday afternoon Sunday School, there was nowhere to hold it except in one of the homes. This was gladly opened, and almost immediately the folks crowded its little rooms to the doors. Classes were often held on the porch and under

197

the trees. A building at Sebastian's Branch was clearly needed.

Hoping to gain the friendship of all who might be interested in a new facility and program for Sebastian's Branch, Sam contacted a local man who had been doing some preaching in the area. He explained that folks needed a center where they could gather for any and all community interests and needs. "I don't mean a church," Sam said, "but a building we can use for Sunday School and any other meetings the folks might want. I'd like your help with the Sunday School."

"Mr. VanderMeer," came the reply, "the Bible says nothing about Sunday School, and since I like to go by the Bible, I'm not interested in having a Sunday School here." But despite this surprising and unfriendly viewpoint, the people remained interested. Before long Mrs. Grace Herald had offered a plot of ground for the building.

"A lease for 99 years," the generous widow said. "No charge at all. Just glad to have you come here to help us."

With volunteer help and materials, money and gifts—a rustic building was soon completed. It is there today on top of a beautiful hill—a lighthouse in that little long forgotten community. We found that one of our young married women, who had learned weaving at Berea College, wanted to weave for us. A loom was found and put in the larger room, and an old mountain art was revived. Now three new looms have been added. Each week a Sunday School is carried on, and the building is open and in use throughout the week with projects encouraging "the abundant life" at Sebastian's Branch.

When Sam sat down to write our annual letter at the very start of the new year in 1969, we did not know that our last Morris Fork Christmas had passed and that the year would unfold in ways that would test us mightily. Yet in his letter, he revealed a deep sense of the need to remember the change—and the bounty—of the many years before. He would not have written out his thoughts and gratitude differently had he known what did lie ahead:

Because there is so much to share you'd better draw your chair up close to the open fire. In fact it is a perfect night to sit by the fire and tell tales because we are having an old-fashioned winter. Last Sunday morning the temperature was 12 degrees below zero and the ground was covered with four inches of soft white snow. The weatherman promises more of the same, so the fireside is doubly welcome.

For unto you is born this day in the city of David, a Saviour which is Christ the Lord. This message of the angel choir took on added meaning this Christmas because we had two funerals in the church. Because a Saviour had been born and redemption made possible, we did not sorrow at those who have no hope. Uncle Sol Riley, one of our most beloved old men who had been the main carpenter in the building of our church, and Letcher Thompson, who for many years served as an elder and co-worker in the church, passed away during the holidays . . .

The various Christmas parties for all age groups were such fun. The primary children loved their games and the hunt for the Magic Candy Tree which had enough peppermint canes for everyone! School age children were most sympathetic when Effie Turner, dressed as Mrs. Santa, interrupted their games and sobbingly told them that Santa had failed to get back home. When she begged them to help her find him they made a wild dash for the outdoors and after much searching, the old fellow, James Morris, was found fast asleep against the barn door. Mrs. Santa scolded, the children yelled with delight, but to no avail. Old Santa was so tired they just couldn't awaken him! When they finally aroused him he was so stiff he couldn't walk. The boys and girls solved this problem by getting the wheel barrow and with much grunting and heaving and some more scolding by Mrs. Santa, they finally got him in the wheel barrow and with shrieks of joy wheeled him to the Sunday school room where they were having their party. He and Mrs. Santa had a joyous reunion and soon the two of them were playing and skipping with the children.

Nola and the mothers made their usual visits to the shut-ins. Ollie Stamper, such a lovely person who has been confined to a wheelchair for many years; Aunt Elizabeth Riley, the widow of Uncle Sol, who is pure sunshine; Aunt Jalia Sebastian, who loves to talk and take care of the preachers, and Aunt Nancy Turner, who is one of the sweetest little grandmothers you ever saw! Mrs. Willie Deaton, an invalid, was so surprised and pleased to be included this year. The last visit was over the mountain to Cow Creek to visit with Granny Mason, the widow of preacher John Mason. Granny Mason loves to read and even though she is past ninety, she is very alert, one of the best quilters in the county, loves the Lord and the fellowship with His people. At all these homes, the women sang carols and gave some of the ''pretties'' you all made possible.

How generously we have been paid, not only during Christmas season, but all through the forty-five years we have been at Morris Fork! We were paid so abundantly at the wonderful Homecoming in July when Dr. Custer Reynolds brought such a wonderful message and the Rev. Chester Ranck led us in such marvelous singing—the voices of our Morris Forkers, who had come home from many states, joining with those who are fortunate enough to still live here. We were paid at our annual Community Fair when the judges from the University of Kentucky compared our several thousand exhibits most favorably with those they had judged at the State Fair. We were extravagantly paid when the University of Kentucky presented us with their highest award, the Sullivan Medallion for outstanding community service. How richly we were paid when young John Edward Eversole and Brenda Sandlin, both High School students, accepted Christ as their Saviour and were baptized and enrolled as members of the church.

Much of our pay has also come from the ex-

Smiles . . . .

A few of our Wooton "Juniors" setting out on a Sunday School "Boosters Day" around 1920.

Sam and I "sit a spell" with Miss McCord on a visit back to Wooton's Creek in 1932.

Sam welcoming Riley Kelley and his family to Sunday School. This photo appeared in a feature article entitled ''Kentucky's Mountain Preacher'' in Presbyterian Life, *August 5, 1950, written by Webb B. Garrison.* (PHOTO BY MACK HUGHES)

Happy Morris Fork faces in front of our campers' cabin.

Eyes and smiles—even the dog's are fixed on "Uncle Sam" in an after church moment. Peter Nai, at center, was a close friend of Jerry Deaton (right) and a frequent "international" visitor.

Jim Cornett joining in some paper plate hat fun with several of us girls and Sam and "Casey" Conklin, stooped at right.

periences young folks from churches all over the United States have had in our summer work camp program, from the vesper services we conduct at the University each year, from the students at Lees Junior College where we have been privileged to teach the New Testament. How true the Word of God is—*Give and it shall be given unto you. With what measure ye mete it shall be measured unto you—good measure—pressed down and running over shall men heap into your bosom.*

> *The fining pot is for silver and the furnace for gold: but the Lord trieth the hearts.*
>
> —Proverbs 17:3

Early spring, 1969, seemed to begin in a typical way at Morris Fork. Winter had passed, one that had been fairly free of serious illnesses or hardships. We began to think of planning for our late spring and summer programs.

The lovely Sarvis trees had already bloomed, and with perhaps just another cool spell or two the dogwood and redbud would also color our hillsides.

In two more years, according to Board rules, Sam and I would have to think of retirement, but not now. It was unlikely, in any case, that we could ever even begin to think of moving away. Our Morris Fork had, with our loving Father's care, grown and changed so marvelously. It had made a part of "Bloody Breathitt" into "Beautiful Breathitt."

All through winter, correspondence had been progressing toward the summer work camps. The usual summer camp programs were just about fully scheduled, and we were to get ready again to visit with young people from all over the church world—strangers to us only for the moment.

Spring Presbytery had announced a meeting in Pikeville. It meant a long drive from Morris Fork, but also a time of fellowship and church business for ministers and elders. Sam planned to go. But the day before, he complained of being dizzy—"feeling sick." This was most unusual for him. Except for one bout with kidney stones, he had never had a sick day. We both had become almost totally immunized through our busyness at work—there was simply no time to be sick! Sam said, "I hope I can go tomorrow, but I'd better call one of the men and ask him to drive. Somehow I don't feel I could drive that long trip."

With a bit of uneasiness, I took his temperature and found it normal, but said, "If you don't feel better in an hour or so, we'll go to Jackson to a doctor." He did feel better, had a good night's sleep, and drove off with one of the elders for the Pikeville meeting. Starting just about daylight, with good driving, they could reach Pikeville, have the meeting, and be home by dusky dark. But all through the day, I worried and wondered, hoping all was well.

Unbeknownst and unplanned, by a most unusual circumstance—though I know now 'twas planned by God—our beloved Dr. Farra VanMeter from Lexington was at this Presbytery meeting. It was a great surprise; no one knew he was coming. When he returned that evening, Sam said, "What do you think? Dr. Van was there, and I took a moment to tell him of my dizzy spell yesterday. He gave me a little goin' over and said, 'I think you've had a mild angina attack. Let someone drive you home. Take these pills and get some extra rest. I think you'll be okay.'"

This brought us all to attention. But Sam insisted he was feeling much better, would get to bed early, and be okay. He did have a good night's sleep. The next morning, he said he wanted to work a bit in the yard, then finish up plans for the Sunday service the next day. He was also making special preparations for the upcoming Memorial Day visitation.

About nine o'clock I answered a telephone call—Dr. VanMeter's voice said, "My nephew wants Sam to come down here to Lexington immediately. He's a heart specialist and wants to see him. Can you be here in a couple of hours?"

I was almost speechless. "Why, Dr. Van," I said, "He's planning to preach tomorrow—he can't come now."

"You're on thin ice," he replied curtly. "Better come right away."

"Of course," I said. "Yes, yes, we'll be right there."

In almost a state of shock I called Sam in, telling him what had happened. He began to object, but I said, "We'll call Tim Jessen in Buckhorn. If he can come tomorrow to preach we'll get ready to go immediately."

It was not as easily done as said, but we did call several neighbors, explaining what was happening, threw a few things together, and were off. I found a neighbor boy to drive . . . just in case.

Then followed almost three weeks of intensive care at Good Samaritan Hospital in Lexington to avoid further serious heart attacks. As I rode home, many, many questions and problems crowded my mind. "How am I going to do it—what can I do?" But again and again the quiet answer came, *Lo, I am with you always . . . All things work together for good to those who serve the Lord . . . I can do all things through Christ who strengthens me.* And I made myself realize that I was not the only one, nor the first, to face such shock.

Everyone rallied at Morris Fork. Ministers of the Presbytery were most wonderfully kind and understanding as they said, "Of course we'll help. We'll take care of everything until Uncle Sam comes back and he must come back, real soon."

Being in a hospital for the very first time was a very new and different experience for Sam, but it did not lessen his daily life of "preaching" and testimony. Before long, he became acquainted with Elizabeth Smith, the maid who took care of his room. She was black, but black or white makes no difference; we are all God's children in need of His forgiveness and love. *He hath made of one blood all nations.*

"Are you a Christian?" Sam asked Elizabeth one morning.

"Yes, sir, I sure am," came the joyful, smiling response—"I love my Saviour."

Each Christmas, after Sam left the hospital, we received a beautiful card from Elizabeth.

Getting back and forth to the hospital, a round trip of 160 miles, was no small part of the "program" that lay ahead. Keeping the community activities going was just about a twenty-four hour job. Good news of Sam's improvement came from the hospital and helped buoy us up . . . but only until the moment came to bring him home.

Dr. Jesse VanMeter was waiting at the hospital. "I had to see you," he said. "I'm dismissing Sam to go to a motel for a week. You know, Nola, if he had ever tried to lead that Memorial Day service, he might have made it up the hill—but he'd have been carried back down.

"Now, I must tell you something else. Sam is going to have to leave Morris Fork. He's making a good recovery, but he cannot continue the load of work there. I have not told him this; we'll have to do that very gently. But I wanted you to know so you could help prepare him."

Help prepare him? How could I? Where to begin?

The Lord is a very present help in time of trouble. Little by little, during our week's stay at the motel, we faced facts, thanking God for His wonderful care and the blessings He still provided.

One of the first things we discussed was the camps. "Of course, we will cancel them—you can't have this responsibility," I said.

"We can't cancel them," came Sam's quick reply. "All the plans are made, and the young people are counting on coming. It's too late for them to make other plans. Each group has its dates, and we just have to stick to that. We can get plenty of help."

In vain I tried to persuade him. I just didn't see how the camps could be possible. There were all the other activities . . . plans for the summer, visitors coming—and our having to prepare to leave Morris Fork! But try to argue with a Dutchman—try to change his plans? No way!

We did get back to Morris Fork, and we did have the campers' programs, along with all the other activities. We lived on the second floor of the Community House. The

209

doctor had said no climbing of steps. So all through that summer, the different campers carried Uncle Sam up and down those steps out of doors so he could be a part of the camping program. He directed things, along with the camp advisors who always came with their groups, from a chair under a shade tree.

One of the biggest mysteries will always be how I got through that summer! All of the visitors, a sick husband, no doctor on whom to lean; activities and programs of the center; getting ready to move with fifty years' accumulation of "stuff" to be disposed of; and all the heartaches of leaving our beloved mountains, our people, our buildings —all that had grown dear and become a part of us from 1927 to 1969. I seemed as though I were in a trance—it wasn't true—just *couldn't* be happening!

But events in our honor at the beginning of October told us—with hugs and tears—that our Morris Fork years were about to end. There was the ceremony as the roadside marker was placed . . . the testimonial dinner at the Buckhorn State Park Lodge . . . the look upon the faces of our dear, dear folks who, like ourselves, could not really say goodbye.

At the end of October, we were ready to leave. No, not ready . . . we would never be ready to leave Morris Fork. We were just trying to accept God's will, not ours.

The last hours were quiet early morning ones; a bit of breakfast with only Grace Post and "Sunday" about. Grace had been such a friend to us, especially after she finished her years of teaching and gave more of her time to helping us keep up with things. Sunday, a very handsome collie, had been with us for five years, ever since the Luddys left him on what they jokingly called a "ninety-nine year leash." He had been a favorite with all the youngsters who came by and was a constant walking companion with Sam. I would always be able to muster a smile remembering the time he was out in the yard, skulking about after he had been completely shorn for treatment of a skin problem. Some of our Morris Forkers came by in a car, and slowed down to inquire after Sam's health. When the lady next to the driver spotted Sunday, she said, " . . . That ain't Lassie, is it?" (Folks had found that name more fittin'.) When I said that indeed it was . . . she responded, "Well! He sure don't favor hisself none, does he?"

With no way or financial means of moving it, we had stacked and stored our accumulation of worldly goods there at the Community House. It was all we could do to carry our heavy hearts, with so many memories stored in them. Folks stayed back, sensing we could not say goodbye without theirs and ours bursting open.

We went out to the car and started down the little road that held countless memories of its own. We took the main highway to Booneville and then headed towards Lexington, believing—as the days ahead would reaffirm—that once more God's promise would be proven.

10
A Golden Twilight

White's Memorial Church and Berea
1970 . . .

Coming to Lexington on this last trip from Morris Fork was quite different from the many other trips we had made there. It seemed like a dream—we were in a maze. When we finally arrived, the big question was "Where do we go now?" There seemed to be no answer. On a missionary salary, it had been impossible to buy and "lay away" a home for retirement—and our Board had made no provisions.

"Oh, we'll find some place in the morning," we said, as we settled into a motel for the night. But the next day we discovered that it was not as easily done. There seemed to be a hopeless search ahead, as day followed anxious day. No luck!

We had been in our motel for several days when we found a note under our door.

"My dad passed away last week," it said. "There is a small cottage here on the farm, and I know if he were here he'd love for you to have it. He was very fond of you, you know. Will you come see it?"

Colonel Johnson had visited us several times. He and his daughter Ann had become good friends, but we had not heard of his death. Of course we did contact Ann immediately. Such a beautiful, beautiful old Kentucky farm we found—and what a wonderful, warm reception from

SAM AND I

Ann and her husband! "The Lord will provide." Colonel Thomas Johnson was a "horse" man, especially interested in jumping horses. All over the walls of the little cottage on the lovely farm in Versailles were pictures of his beautiful horses.

Sam and I had a year and a month or so in the little cottage. His health improved steadily. We were so happy and grateful for this . . . in spite of our constant grief and our longing to be "back home."

We were especially happy when Sam was well enough to accept calls to fill Sunday pulpit vacancies in some of the nearby churches of Lexington and Versailles; it was good for him to be at least a bit "in harness" again.

Suddenly, out of a blue sky, came a letter from White's Memorial Presbyterian Church, a small country church

213

about four miles out of Berea. "We need a pastor," they wrote. "Would you consider coming to our church?"

"Why, of course not," Sam said to me immediately. "If I were able to have a church, I'd go right back to Morris Fork. I just can't do this." So he wrote them, expressing his regrets and thanking them for the invitation.

But "God's ways are not our ways . . . His ways are past finding out." In a very short time, a second letter came. "We have not had a pastor for a long time," it said. "Students have been coming from the Seminary, but we need a regular man, someone to be here, to live in our manse. Won't you please come talk with us?"

"Well," said Sam. "Maybe the Lord is having something to do with this; maybe I'd better go talk with them." So a date was set to meet some of the folks at the church.

A large group turned out to welcome us. After prayer and much good heart-to-heart talk, we agreed to come to White's, if, as Sam told them, they were sure they wanted "an old man."

For five years we had such a happy and bountiful ministry amongst new and good friends. How wonderfully the Lord provided for a golden twilight together. We had not expected to be "in the saddle" again . . . well, nearly so! Through White's Memorial, and residing on the edge of Berea, we were able to enjoy the fellowship and opportunities of Berea College. How Sam loved the chance to work with young people again. He was invited to give the College Baccalaureate in 1972. No occasion in his life meant more to him than this.

About a year later, Johnny VanderMeer and his wife came up from Florida to help us complete the celebration of Homecoming Week, a White's Memorial tradition. Johnny came in response to a special invitation from Sam, who wanted to introduce him to some of the "old timers" of the church who had been avid fans of "The Dutch Master," who had pitched two consecutive no-hitters for the Cincinnati Reds of the Thirties.

Johnny wrote to remind me how, during the visit, he had done some hospital rounds with Sam. "I visited patients with him on two mornings. I was amazed; everyone knew him. I couldn't tell who wanted to see him the most . . . patients, nurses, doctors or visitors. In all my own forty years of travel, I had not seen such love shown so clearly to anyone."

THE REFINING POT

On the 17th of July, a Thursday night in 1975, we went to a county agricultural meeting in Berea where Sam had a part in the program. It was a short evening and so it was not too late when we got to bed.

In the morning, after a good night's sleep, Sam said, "It's not too hot today. There are a few more blackberries I'd like to get. Not many left . . . this will be the last picking. I won't be gone too long."

"Remember, we're having a visitor for supper," I replied, "so don't get too tired."

He came back a bit before noon and had a bit o' lunch. Then he said, "Think I'll lie down for a little nap, then help you finish up with dinner."

About two o'clock, I went to the bedroom. He complained of pain in his arm, something that had happened many times since the first attack. I gave him a nitroglycerine tablet, which the doctor had left. At two thirty I was back in the bedroom. Not a sound had come from him, but he said his arm still hurt, so I gave him another tablet and went back to my dinner preparations.

When I came back about three, I couldn't believe my eyes. In total shock, I screamed, "Oh, no!" He was gone, not a sound, not a call, not a goodbye! All was so unbelievable!

We had celebrated our 48th anniversary in June, looking forward to our 50th. We were so much a part of each other's lives, our church, our community, our home—. We did everything together. The only thing I remember that Sam never did was ironing, or mending his socks, although he did sew on buttons.

It seems he must be here . . . as I prepare a meal, come

215

into the house, get ready for Sunday School and services, and want advice for so many, many things.

But these days I'm learning more and more, *Let not your heart be troubled; The soul that on Jesus hath leaned for repose, He will not, He will not desert to his foes. That soul, though all hell should endeavor to shake, He'll never, no never, no never forsake.*

And I saw a new heaven and a new earth . . . And God shall wipe away all tears from their eyes, and there will be no more death, neither sorrow nor crying. God's promises are true.

Some months after his passing, I found among some of Sam's books and papers the text of a sermon he had written out rather fully and dated March, 1927—three months before our marriage. Over fifty years later, its last words took on very deep and special meaning:

"Let us thank God that He has given us a clear vision of our danger, possessions, responsibilities and our security, and may He help us to be obedient to the 'Heavenly vision.'"

During the memorial service for Sam at the little Morris Fork church, the minister announced "A memorial for Uncle Sam has been given here and since we needed a new organ, we purchased that as his memorial. He was so interested in good music, I am happy to say we owe only $500.00 to finish payment for our organ—I know that will come this year."

After the service, there was a community dinner in the church yard. Just before returning thanks, the minister said "I have an announcement—our offering this morning was $500.00"—Many people crowded the little church that day—The young people who had had to leave to "make a living" had come home—and this was their tribute to Uncle Sam's memory.

11
A Quilt for Sam

"... a most precious experience ..."

... the church was filled with mountain people—his people. At the time for the sermon, the present pastor, Alan McCraine, asked any who wished to speak a word. One by one, people rose to speak simply of the witness Sam had made to them, praising God for sending him to tell them of a Savior. Afterward, we gathered on the sunny lawn for dinner on the ground, which people had brought with them. There we talked into the afternoon about God's mercies to all of us. It was a most precious experience I shall never forget.

—Reverend Jack Weller
Author of *Yesterday's People*

"They only needed a friend . . ."

Part of the fun for Uncle Sam had to be the introduction of his new-fangled notions to the skeptical mountain people. It is, of course, characteristic of folks who live in the country to enjoy the fun of practical jokes—and of the spectacle of someone's being fooled. And if there is a sense of good will and respect among a group of men—then no one really minds when the turn to be guffawed at falls on him. And in that group of Morris Fork men—who could have been in Vermont, or Kansas—each would get to be known for something. One would be the best storyteller, one would be the best stone cutter, one would be a mender of harness, one would be the most thoughtful. In that Morris Fork group, Sam was the one who always "sprung" something new. Oh, he was more—in the wider context of church, school and whole community—but in the informal group of men who enjoyed being together, he was the idea person.

And they all looked forward to the laugh at the end. It meant that they had taken some foolish bits of pipe and fittings, and made a pump for a second-floor kitchen sink, and it worked . . . it meant that they had strung up on chains some plain old wagon wheels— ridiculous!—to see them transformed into light fixtures (candle holders, then) which became another perfect part of the whole creation of their church . . . it meant that they had spent a good day not in the corn field but digging scraggly bushes out of the woods, carting them to open spaces near the church, where months later folks would stop, to marvel at the blooms they had walked over and past all their lives.

Sam's ideas didn't disrupt their lives, beat them down, inflame them to anger, or promise them utopia —here or hereafter. He just helped them to see what could be done with what they had before their eyes and inside their heads, so that they observed everything around and about with a sharp new sense of potential. He himself never ceased to wonder at all there is to work with; he had a fine artistic sense of usefulness and beauty that wrought many a transfor-

218

mation for people who were lucky enough to spend time around him. "Amazing!" was one of his favorite exclamations.

And what he must have enjoyed the most, as they laughed at the look on Uncle Sol Riley's face, when the water gushed through the pump for the first time, or when dubious Jim Cornett enjoyed the man who came to "teach us how to play?"—so much so he offered him his mule for a ride to the station—"if you have to go . . . "—was that now these men knew that some barrier of hopelessness had been broken, that something good, positive, light, worthwhile, could come into their lives *by their own doing.*

These mountain men, who would be laughed at in Lexington, who would be called "ignorant" or "backward," needed no self-congratulating missionary who saw himself as God's gift to the hills. They only needed a friend, a man "just like us" who could give and take a joke, and who—every now and then—had a crazy idea that worked.

—Judy Luddy
1980

"How Fortunate I Was . . . "

In August of 1978, J. Garber Drushal, who had recently retired as President of the College of Wooster, took a few moments to recall his acquaintance with Sam during the years he was growing up in Lost Creek, where his father and mother guided the Riverside mission school and church:

> Uncle Sam was in our home on numerous occasions before his marriage. One time was for a Christian Endeavor convention. At that time, he asked me to write the C. E. notes for the area, a kind of news of the mountains with comments from the point of view of youth in high school. My first reaction was that I was not talented enough, too young, or some such . . . I do not recall how many times I wrote the C. E. notes, but Uncle Sam would send them out and give me credit. It not only encouraged me to write . . . but applied a leadership principle to me which I have never forgotten: always try to get young people to do more than they thought they could and do it better than they expected. In working with college students for over forty years, I tried to apply that principle.
>
> During recent years, when as president I addressed the freshmen their first week on campus, I tried to let them know what we expected more of them than they planned . . . On one such occasion, as I walked back to the office, I distinctly remember recalling to myself: "How fortunate I was that Sam VanderMeer walked part of the way with me on the path of my life."

" . . . Sam VanderMeer Was Able to Sit Where They Sat."

Although the drive, in his Dodge Dart, over the winding and hilly road to Jackson, was not an easy one—even on modern pavement—Sam looked forward to each class of his Bible course at Lees College. He loved being with young students, instilling in them his own passion for learning. The College, like Berea later, valued him especially for his teaching and counseling insight. Like everyone else also, they just plain enjoyed his company.

Lees President, Troy Eslinger, first met Sam when he came to visit the Presbyterian Seminary in Louisville in either the fall of 1950 or the spring of 1951:

> . . . A fellow student, John de Kruyter, had invited Sam to conduct a series of services at the Fern Creek Presbyterian Church, of which John was then Pastor. The fact that Sam himself was not a seminary graduate did not prevent him from captivating a majority of the seminary students on the day he spoke at the campus chapel. Several, like myself, determined then and there that here was a man peculiarly chosen by God for a ministry to people of virtually all levels—from the hill country of east Kentucky to the sophisticated environs of a seminary student body. . . .

> When, during the middle to late 1960's, Sam accepted an invitation from me to join the staff at Lees as Bible Instructor, our relationships became even more close. It would be impossible to relate all of the many experiences of that period. However, there is one that must be reported.

> Sometime late in the fall, before cold weather set in, Sam and Nola invited the College faculty and their families out to Morris Fork for a picnic. And, since the church building at Morris Fork is at the very heart of the community center there, and further, since life itself was for Sam and Nola a devotional experience, it was completely natural that before leaving, the College

group found itself assembled in the church for a few moments of worship.

As a part of his extemporary comments, Sam related one of the special discoveries he had made since joining the Lees College faculty. He told us about a meeting in the recreation room at the College, in which at first his seat was located in such a position that when he looked at a painting on one of the walls, it appeared as only a framed canvas with globs of paint stretching across the surface. It was not until later in the day, when he sat in another position, that he could see and more fully appreciate the true beauty of that painting. He said, "It then dawned on me that here was a parable of the classroom. If the instructor is to be able to communicate effectively with his students, he must first know where they sit. And to do that must sit where they sit." This approach to instruction has been strongly emphasized at Lees ever since that time!

In a most remarkable fashion, Sam VanderMeer was able to "sit where they sat," whether "they" were college students, families of the hill country, college faculty and staff, or sophisticated business and professional leaders.

To know him and to be with him was to experience renewal within one's own self.

"... I Shall Cherish That Scrap of Paper and That Memory As Long As I Live."

After Sam's passing, Shirley Aldenderfer—a member of our White's Memorial congregation—wanted me to have the thoughts that had come to her, and so she sent them on to me:

It was a very warm evening in early summer when I first set eyes on the little church along Route 1983—Berea. My husband had taken the children and myself out for a drive along this delightful back country road, overgrown with tiger lilies and honeysuckle. Around a bend, we came upon it, standing out like a beacon in the dimming twilight. Across the road, on a bank edging the lawn, and everywhere around the ranch-style brick house, flowers of every kind and color grew with determined profusion.

"My word!" I exclaimed. "It looks like the garden of Eden!" Whoever tends this place, I thought, certainly has got either two green thumbs or a rather direct connection with God. It didn't take me long to discover that both of my thoughts were true.

The following Sunday, I visited the church with our friends, Bob and Helen Sloe. They had discovered White's Memorial earlier and had been excited to learn that its minister, Sam VanderMeer, was the very same man of God who had made such a deep impression on their daughter at a summer work camp in the Kentucky mountains quite a few years earlier.

Even in his later years—when we came to know him—"Uncle Sam" was a strong man, powerful of build. But he was also a man of gentle persuasion who always made you feel good about yourself and about life. When he shook your hand, it was with a firm, confident clasp that told you instantly, "I'm delighted to know you." It seemed as though he could see into your innermost being and put to use for the good of the community the newly- found interests or talents he had just discovered.

"Saminola" had been the spiritual leaders of White's Memorial for four or five years by the time we arrived on the scene. They had taught the members of a waning church to be aware of their community, and to contribute to the welfare of their distant neighbors as well as those close by.

Uncle Sam gave an air of "hominess" to White's Memorial. His greeting each Sunday was a welcome to a cheerful hearth.

What lingers most in my memory is the time he persuaded me to play for a small wedding of two out-of-town students. I practiced faithfully for weeks in order to be well-prepared for the event. Whenever I arrived at the church, Uncle Sam was either there, working about, or there was evidence of his having been there. One afternoon, I found placed on top of the organ a coffee can filled with beautiful, fragrant roses. It was accompanied by a note scribbled in familiar script:

Dear Shirley,
    Please take us home with you. We are so lonely growing here among the parsley.

The Roses

I shall cherish that scrap of paper and that memory as long as I live.

A big moment for Uncle Sam at White's was his surprise 75th birthday celebration. "The Old Ground Hog" (he joked about his February 2nd birthdate) was lured to a Saturday night supper that turned into "This is Your Life, Uncle Sam." During the evening, he was gifted with a new suit which he never claimed to need. He'd rather have put the money into a building fund. Uncle Sam had great dreams for White's Memorial, as he had had them for Morris Fork. He longed for the congregation to begin an expansion program that would afford some much-needed space for the Sunday School which was growing along with the congregation.

A sorrowful moment in Uncle Sam's ministry at White's was the funeral for Oscar Harrison, the revered patriarch of our congregation. Mr. Harrison had been a great personal friend and inspiration, and Uncle Sam mourned his loss. Two weeks later, the congregation mourned for Uncle Sam.

"He walked straight and careful . . . "

In the autumn after Sam's passing, a very touching letter came one morning in the mail. It was postmarked Lexington and dated November 23:

My Dearest Mrs. Nola

I just knew about our Dear Rev Vandermere departer from this troubled world and going to the Fathers Kingdom . . . Rev Sam was a fine and great christian . . . He walked straight and careful and I do hope there will be many folks to follow in his step.

Mr and Mrs McKinnicy of Berea he's a mail man, they were by to see me on Nov. 19th and that how I knew about Rev Sam for I ask them about you all. it really hit me a terrible blow. Please take care of you self. I can never forget you, for your loving Kindness to me in the pass 7 or 8 years. I have been helped an awful lot by you. God Bless you always.

Fondly, Elizabeth J Smith

"To God be the glory"

Sam is gone now, but a spirit
Pervades his haunts mid hills and hollows.
Words he spoke are oft repeated,
His acts and deeds are taught and copied.
Just as the trees he planted grow rings, expanding,
So the widening circle of his influence
Touches life and persons far away.
The many he has loved and influenced
Have spread abroad to touch and influence
Life and people wherever they chance to be.
Sam would say "To God be the glory."

—Mary Scott Moore, Breathitt County,
Home Demonstration Agent
University of Kentucky

" . . . Men sensed that God was with him."

Samuel VanderMeer was a gift of the Netherlands and of the Dutch Reformed Church to Eastern Kentucky and to the Presbyterian Church. It was surely in the providence of God that such a gift came to be given. He sought neither Eastern Kentucky nor the ministry in the Presbyterian Church, but they sought him; and they pursued him until they possessed him. Coming within the bounds of the Presbytery of Buckhorn for a summer, he shortly became a part of it and of its successors for a lifetime. Neither he nor the Presbytery could have known what was ahead in terms of fruitful ministry when he was ordained to the Gospel Ministry on April 14, 1927, at the age of twenty-seven.

Our beloved brother in Christ was a friend to all—to God and to man, to old and to young, to rich and to poor, to city and to country, as also to us. He had a loving heart, a quickened conscience, a surrendered will, a savory humor, and an appreciative disposition. Because of these, he could preach, or reprove, or counsel, or comfort, or simply converse; and men sensed that God was with him.

—Excerpt—Resolution of the Presbytery of Transylvania (Union) September 4, 1975

12
"Continuance"

No one knew that a good garden needed tending better than Sam did. It would please him to know that the garden of abundant activity at Morris Fork has been tended . . . faithfully and well.

Caroling still fills the winter air up and down those blessed hills each Christmas, and the Women's Group carries on with considerable activity.

During a visit in 1978, it thrilled me to learn that the Bible School of the upcoming summer would have an enrollment of over a hundred youngsters and that it would include a lunch program for all.

With considerable interest from many families, the camper tradition has been enhanced by young Morris Forkers going outside to help others elsewhere. One group has helped to paint a country church in Maine. Think of it! How Sam would have loved to be a part of that expedition! It was the sort of outreach and sharing he had inspired.

One of our last projects at Morris Fork had been the encouragement of interest in creating a special spot where many examples of the crafts of our area could be placed for Morris Fork grandchildren—and for visitors—to see. The old schoolhouse, no longer used for school, was purchased from the county and donated to Morris Fork by Grace Post. It is now the Grace Post Memorial Craft Shop.

Sam was very excited when Sophie Deaton donated the old family cabin, that had been on Freeman Fork, for such a use. A wonderful Morris Fork day was built around the occasion of the log raisin', as our men re-erected the little cabin and hand cut and put in place new wood shakes for its roof. I remember what fun it was seeing Aunt Sally Riley there in her pretty long dress and bonnet—as she moved through all the festivity.

With the very dedicated help of Tim Long, a great interest in creating a Morris Fork Crafts Center was developed. And with the guidance of Pastor John Kidd, the work of our local folks now makes its way to distant homes and horizons.

Even before the coming of World War II, some of our folks, the younger ones especially, left Morris Fork in the hope of finding work opportunities. This was a real wrench for us and for them. But without roads, industries could not get anywhere near us nor really prosper in our undeveloped countryside.

With help from the Extension Department of the University, the County and Home Agents, much improvement had been made with the little farms. Improved crops followed rotation and better fertilizing; but even this did not afford a real livelihood.

Many of the young folks had gone on to high school and college, but jobs were not forthcoming. So on to other parts of Kentucky, Ohio, Michigan, and even Florida, they went, never forgetting the old mountain refrain, "O those hills, those beautiful hills . . . " we often sang. Governor Bert Combs used to joke that you could be in the mountains on a Sunday and tell when a traffic light changed in Dayton!

A good many folks were teachers. Some were bankers, or worked in a plant. But they were forced to go away from their beloved hills—into a different world. We had tried to make some preparation for this, for we knew life could not go on forever in the isolated hills, but how could we really prepare our folks for such a change! Life outside was all so vastly different from the sheltered life of the isolated hills. Such constant noise on every hand—the buzzing of countless vehicles and machinery—hordes of people—the demand to be "on time"—the restrictions, rules, regulations—the flat, dirty cities, with no mountains! So hard to make such an adjustment; and many found they could not do it. Some found unfriendliness or even got into serious trouble in the far different city life.

"Ohio is running over with mountain folks—we don't like them."

"That's okay," came the answer, "we don't like you either."

One family was having an especially hard time. Tossing one night, unable to sleep, Sarah said to her husband, "Jim, if I was to die, where would you put me?"

"Hush, honey," he replied. "Don't have such talk."

"But I mean it," she persisted. "I want to know—I'm not jokin'. Where would you take me?"

"Why, you know—right back to Long's Creek, of course."

After a bit more twisting and turning, she sat up in bed. "Jim," she said, "would you just as soon take me back home alive as dead?"

Leaving Cincinnati, they came "home" in a hurry.

Some other folks have returned as well, or at least have decided to hold onto their bit of Morris Fork, even with the great coal shovels about to peer over their beloved hills.

And it's not all dark with those who have left. We were happy to have a letter from a minister in Middletown, Ohio, who said, "Yesterday six of your Morris Forkers joined our church. It's just a shot in the arm to see such fine Christian young people take their place in another part of our Lord's vineyard. Thank you for sending them to us."

One day, in the early years, Sam separated a couple of boys fighting in the school yard. One had a knife. "Let me have that knife," Sam said. "When you are old enough to have it, I'll give it back to you."

About twenty-five years later, Sam was speaking in a

Cincinnati church. After the service, a nicely dressed gentleman came to him saying, "I have a good job in the bank here, and I'm an elder in this church. I'd like you to meet my friends. Could you go to the bank with me tomorrow?"

Looking at him, a bit puzzled, Sam said, "Why yes, I'll be glad to go with you."

After guiding him through the bank and introducing him to the president, the young man put his arm on Sam's shoulder saying, "Thank you, Uncle Sam; you can give me back my knife now. I think I know what to do with it."

As "our children" came back for vacations or weekends from their various jobs in Ohio—Indiana—or wherever, the love and loyalty of their beloved mountain homes was still deep in their hearts. These hills would always be home; they never really "settled down" in the big city.

One Sunday, after the service, one of our visiting boys handed Sam an envelope. To his amazement, when he opened it, he found five hundred dollars!

"Why, Walter," Sam exclaimed, "this must be a whole month's salary. You can't afford to give this."

"I want to give it to the church," Walter answered, "and I can't afford to give less, when I remember all the church and Morris Fork have done for me."

Every twice in a while, such wonderful things happened . . . and still happen.

When I was at the Lexington airport, bound for New England and some final work on this little volume, I had a happy surprise reunion with Ray Cornett. Ray and his wife had just finished a good visit with the home folks at Morris Fork and were on their way back to their own home in Florida.

Ray spoke of his thirty-four years with Delta Airlines—he is their personnel manager in Tampa—and of the wonderful opportunities he had had to travel all over the world. But he wanted to remember . . . and to talk most about the long ago year when Sam had made arrangements for him to go to Farm School. "It was hard to

230

be away from home, but I'm glad I stuck it out and graduated," he said. "I go back every year for our alumni meeting."

There was so much to talk about that we didn't have a minute to remember the time that Ray carried the postcard to the 4-H meeting in Lexington—and brought it all the way back to me at Morris Fork!

I remember what my little friend at Wooton had said about her grandchild. "Hits got sense, but hits got to learn how to use that sense."

In December of 1941, just three days before Pearl Harbor, Sam wrote a letter that went out to many of our supporting friends and churches. In it he said:

> One cannot help but wonder about the future of a community like Morris Fork. Most of the timber has been cut, the land worn out, families living closer together, no industries. Our young people whom we send out for their education find no incentive to return—except of course that this is home—but there are no means of a livelihood for them, so they go off to the cities where they marry city folks and are thus definitely out of the picture as far as future residence goes. We have been pleased with the type of person they marry and most of them seem to carry on the traditions which the Church gave them. Maybe our task is simply the laying of Christian foundations.
>
> We are not marking time by any means—our program is going full swing and He who has led us this far will continue to lead us on. Who knows what He may have in store for us? This is His work and these are His people . . .

But it was much later—in the handwritten yellow sheets he left behind—that Sam somehow captured the essence of Morris Fork and all of our own abundant years there . . . in the mountains:

> Late one Sunday afternoon riding my big horse,

Silver, down the steep mountainside, as the sun was hiding behind the tall hills plunging into the deep valley, nearing the little log cabin where Aunt Nell Riley lived, I saw her standing by one of the slim poles that supported the porch roof. Aunt Nell's life had not been an easy one but she had what Uncle John B. Lewis called "that rare quality of continuance." Coming up to her porch, I saw the wonderful smile that always came so readily to her lovely wrinkled face. She greeted me with the usual salutation, "Howdy, get down and come in." Because it was nearing the edge of dark, I told her that I had to get home to do up the chores. Then with a mist in her clear blue eyes she said, "I want you to take this here package to Miss Noley 'cause I've been a studyin how good she has been to me and my younguns." I thanked her and rode on down the creek to my home. I found Nola in the kitchen preparing supper and as I handed her the little parcel I told her about my conversation with Aunt Nell. The gift was wrapped in a crumpled page from a catalogue. Inside we found one thin dime—and a used handkerchief which she had washed and ironed. Our eyes became blurred as we looked upon Aunt Nell's gift of love and gratitude—a lovely miniature of God's great gift of love which was wrapped in crumpled swaddling clothes and laid in a manger. We found our hearts strangely moved and warmed by her gift, even as our hearts have been warmed over and over again during the years we have had the privilege of serving God and our mountain people.

I've been a studyin'—Looking back over the forty some odd years spent in the Kentucky mountains it is amazing the number of times that same expression has been heard. Uncle Lewis Deaton used it when I went to see him one day when he was in bed with a prolonged illness. Uncle Lewis was a most colorful individual who seemed to be absolutely fearless of man or beast. His home was one of the best on the creek and in his stable he always had the finest stock. His farm, his house and in fact everything he had was always the best. He loved good horses and was an excellent rider. Uncle Lewis was proud of the fact that he had never been indicted in the courts. For many years he was an officer of the law, hating law violators, liquor and as he called them, "Sorry, no account people." On one occasion seeing some "no account" young men disturbing a meeting he said, "Those dirty-eared, cow-faced things." Because of his sharp tongue he was often called 'Wasper.' One Sunday riding down to Crockettsville to an out station Sunday School, Uncle Lewis reached over and handed me a half dollar. I said, "What's that for?" and he responded, "That's for that good sarmint you preached this morning against the sorry, no-count folks." Although his tongue could be very sharp at times, there was also a gentleness about him that became more obvious as he grew older, especially after he became bedfast. During his prolonged illness we spent a great deal of time with him. He constantly reminded us of his good record and felt that because of this God would accept him, never realizing that in the sight of God all our righteousness is as filthy rags. Then one day the truth broke upon him that he was a sinner and Christ had died for him and that God accepted him not because of his good record, but because he was trusting in Christ as his Savior. During this last illness on one of our many visits, I cut the last rose of the season from our garden and took it to Uncle Lewis. He was lying on the bed in the lower room of Mary Thompson's house. The door to his room was open; as he saw me in the doorway holding in my hand this "last rose" his face lighted up with a smile of pleasure. "I've been layin' here a studyin' about how good everybody has been to me," he said. Then pointing to a little stand table by his bedside he said, "Looky here—Clay Smith sent me them biscuits, Lily the peppermint candy, Marthy the jar of honey—and now you come a bringin' me a rose—I'm just abilin' over with pure satisfaction."

SAM AND NOLA OF MORRIS FORK

Samuel VanderMeer came here from New Jersey in 1923. "Uncle Sam" to generations of Ky. youngsters, he became pastor of the Morris Fork Presbyterian Church in 1927, the year he married nurse Nola Pease. Missionaries, community builders. They gave a total of 98 years of service and love to this area, until retirement in 1969. Church and Community Center. 1 mile.

Epilogue

Like the few phrases of tribute that are cut into the marble of the Lincoln Memorial, these words—on a bronze highway marker near Booneville, Kentucky—give simple summary to the extraordinary. As with that other Kentuckian, they leave much more to be remembered, and told, elsewhere. To be "enshrined forever" in the hearts of those they served was not a conscious goal of Sam and Nola VanderMeer. It was simply the inevitable essence of how they lived, and of what they lived for.

Born thousands of miles apart, Samuel VanderMeer and Nola Pease might have lived out their lives at an even greater distance from each other. But they were brought together to become Uncle Sam and Aunt Nola of Morris Fork. Their eyes were lifted up unto the Kentucky hills, and great strength came to them.

The quilt of mountain memories that has been unfolded here is a chronicle of Christian achievement. At Morris Fork alone, Sam and Nola rose to the work and the promise of more than fifteen thousand days. Only a fraction of the whole of these days—each with its measure of accomplishment and frustration—has been made visible here.

Nothing disturbed Sam and Nola more than the fact that those who sought to tell the mountain story at one time or another passed over the work of those numerous dedicated missionaries who had come, not to frighten with fire and brimstone, but to serve and care and labor. Surely the preceding pages have done much to redress that oversight.

At Morris Fork, the church ministered wide and deep: wide to nutrition, education, agriculture; to skill, citizenship and aspiration; deep to pain and grief, love and joy. Aunt Nola and Uncle Sam were always ready to learn as well as teach and, in behalf of their Lord, to receive as well as give. They ministered to—not down to. The language of each was the language of example and deed.

Sam had an inherent distaste for being called "Reverend," but he expected visiting preachers to dress as well for the Morris Fork congregation as they did for their prosperous suburban ones. He knew, however, that among other things, God is a farmer . . . and has a sense of humor. Standing there in the pulpit one Sunday morning, in his dark suit and tie, Sam asked for a birthday gift of manure for his garden!

No one ever "joshed" more people into tasting the inner and outer goodness of life, "joshed" them into reverence, than did Sam VanderMeer. Without his smiles, and those of his tireless helpmate, the tired country would not have smiled. Its transformation from a place of frequent violence and constant isolation to a community of peace and new horizons was their conscious translation of John 10:10 . . . "I am come that they might have life, and that they might have it more abundantly."

By the middle years of their work at Morris Fork, public recognition began to come from all across Kentucky. In 1950 Centre College conferred upon Sam the honorary degree of Doctor of Divinity. The citation quite appropriately made reference to both members of the VanderMeer team.

The Kentucky Golden Sheaf Award "for distinguished service to agriculture and rural living" was given to Sam in 1963. "All of us are basking in your reflected glory," Thomson Bryant, a former administrator in the University's Cooperative Extension Program wrote. "You will live on," he continued, "long after your demise, in the lives of the boys and girls you have helped and encouraged . . . you just keep on keeping on." And of course Sam did.

Five years later, at commencement exercises in Lexington, the University conferred upon Sam its highest honor: The Sullivan Medallion, presented "to those who show a spirit of love for and helpfulness to others." Neither the little Dutch boy who had come to America as a humble toddler, nor the little brown-eyed girl who had grown up on the freezing and thawing of Michigan and Minnesota, could have known that such a time would await them.

But none of these honors held such deep meaning as that which came on the eve of retirement from Morris Fork in 1969. In that heart-filled hour, Sam and Nola were presented with a bound collection of personal letters of loving appreciation, many of them humbly and touchingly handwritten. I have never held a more moving book.

For Uncle Sam, holding it was to perhaps feel again the rough handshakes of the men whose lives he had affected deeply . . . men like Zack Yeary, who crossed miles of mountain ridges on foot each day to work alongside him. Such men wept for their loss, while rejoicing in his certain victory, when he died.

For Aunt Nola, walking briskly toward her ninetieth birthday, it is to hold again her countless babies, now of all ages, and to hear again the laughter of the Morris Fork girls washing the school lunch kettles in the yard.

Tireless though they were, these two missionaries could, on occasion, frown or sputter very humanly about something going on around them. I recall that they did not like having to see and hear a motor bike, purchased and fueled by a federal welfare check, carrying its aimless passenger up and down the road which had been built by hand, and used so often for better ends. Nor did they like to hear that some government program was seeking to train a Morris Forker, already skilled in stonemasonry, to become a landscape gardener!

On occasion, a small spark would fly when the busyness of one grazed against the busyness of the other. They were not immune to the tensions or frustrations that come with the great commitment of energy, long day upon long day. But they never lapsed into self-pity or self-indulgence. They never seemed to take anger out on anyone; it's easy to imagine that a garden row might have been hoed a bit vigorously, or some bread dough punched down with a vengeance, but nothing turned inward to smolder, or flared out to hurt and scar. They were not moody or unpredictable, and they always kept that deeper composure and commitment.

When Conrad Feltner sat down to recall his many arduous treks to Morris Fork, during his years as a county extension agent, he remembered that moment all of us who were fortunate enough to visit there would always remember:

> "When we rounded the corner to get our first view of Morris Fork, it seemed that all of our troubles, and the weather and everything else, were forgotten, because there was something special about Morris Fork and Sam and Nola that made you always want to return."

The spell of Morris Fork—cast again in these pages—was the spell of those clear and beautiful lines of the Shaker melody . . .

> "'Tis a gift to be simple,
> 'Tis a gift to be free,
> 'Tis a gift to come down where you ought to be.
> And when you find yourself
> In the place just right,
> You'll be in the valley of love and delight."

The waters of the little creek called Morris Fork flow slowly across their limestone bed into those of Long's Creek. Joining these, they flow to the Middle Fork of the Kentucky River and on to the Kentucky itself. Across a

238

varied landscape of deep gorges crossed by Daniel Boone, and of the bluegrass and bustling commerce beyond, the Kentucky moves to the Father of Waters . . . and to the great swells and depths of the oceans.

For more than a half century now, the spiritual head-waters of Morris Fork have flowed forth. The spirit of Morris Fork has been carried in the hearts and hands of people, to places as near as Booneville . . . Jackson and Traveller's Rest . . . and as far as Africa and beyond.

It has been quite an experience for me . . . this quilt making. In that wonderful way she has always had of keeping "guesties" from the sin of laziness . . . by having them up 'n doing as she crisscrossed the kitchen herself a hundred times, Aunt Nola has kept me piecing and sewing. When I have slumbered, or strayed to other things, I have always felt that she was forgiving about it, but that she was "praying me back" to something important that needed doing and that wanted finishing. I have never been with her for very long during these past few years when I haven't looked at her hands and thought of all the paring knives, bridles, bandages, chickens, sticks of wood, hands, hymnals, Christmas packages, mixing bowls, babies . . . and prayers . . . they have held.

You have finished the book which Uncle Sam began, Aunt Nola, and in Deuteronomy is your benediction.

"For the Lord thy God hath blessed thee,
In all the works of thy hand."

—Frederick L. Luddy

THE PRAYER BELL

Far down the fork and up the glade
And into every little dell,
At sunset, rings for man and maid,
The loved prayer bell.

Then, on the lowland, on the hill,
In wood or field they hear it well.
And pause a moment, rapt and still
While rings the bell.

The woodman lays his keen ax down,
The traveller halts, beneath the spell,
As up from the creek to wooded crown,
Peals out the bell.

A mood of worship fills the air,
And heaven breathes, where once was hell.
While all the valley stands at prayer,
And hears the bell.

—Dr. Charles Zarbaugh